The Limits of Econometrics

To Angela and John

The Limits of Econometrics

Adrian C. Darnell and J. Lynne Evans

Edward Elgar

Published by
Edward Elgar Publishing Limited
Gower House
Croft Road
Aldershot
Hants GUll 3HR
England

Gower Publishing Company
Old Post Road
Brookfield
Vermont 05036
USA

British Library Cataloguing in Publication Data
Darnell, A.C. (Adrian C.)
    The limits of econometrics.
    1. Econometrics
    I. Title II. Evans, J. Lynne
    330'. 028

Library of Congress Cataloging-in-Publication Data
Darnell, A.C.
    The limits of econometrics / Adrian C. Darnell and
J. Lynne Evans.
      p. cm.
    Includes bibliographical references.
    1. Econometrics. I. Evans, Lynne. II. Title.
HB139.D36 1990
330'.01'5195–dc20
90–2798
CIP

ISBN 1–85278–048–7
ISBN 1–85278–517–9 pbk

Printed in Great Britain by
Billing & Sons Ltd, Worcester

Contents

Preface

Many economists appear to have lost some confidence in econometrics and econometricians; it is also apparent that many econometricians have attempted to erect econometrics as a separate discipline in its own right, or even as an umbrella discipline for economics. This text seeks to establish the appropriate role which econometrics should play. To achieve this ambitious aim, the limits of econometric investigations will be identified through a critical appraisal of each of the 'packages' on offer. Essentially there appear to be five distinct packages: the 'traditional' approach, those of, respectively, Professors Hendry; Leamer; and Sims; and the increasingly popular approach of 'cointegration'.

This book is aimed both at general economists and at practising econometricians. It does not seek to present highly technical econometric theory, rather we offer critical descriptions of the competing 'approaches' using as low a level of technical language as possible. We seek to identify what econometrics can offer in the attempt to further our understanding of economic phenomena.

During the 1960s, many had hoped that econometrics would provide a sound 'scientific' foundation for economics, along the lines of the standard hard science model of, for example, physics. Much of that anticipation may be attributed to a misunderstanding of the methodology of economic enquiry, and especially to a misunderstanding of the methodological status of econometrics; the hope was certainly fuelled by the writings of the 'positivists' and the 'operationalists' and those who espoused these rather fashionable labels (such as Friedman in his 'Essay on the methodology of positive economics' (1953) and Lipsey's best-selling undergraduate text *An Introduction to Positive Economics* (first edition 1963)). The optimism was, and is, misplaced; however, the appropriate response to the dissatisfaction (both with regard to the 'worth' of econometrics and with regard to economics in general) which has recently been articulated is not to discard either methodology or econometrics. We wish, here, to offer a better understanding of the role which econometrics can play within the discipline of economics, and will attempt to do so by offering some methodological observations on the currently popular applied econometric strategies. In so doing, we address the claims made by the proponents of the different approaches and seek to re-establish a role for the 'traditional' approach which has been so heavily criticized by those who propose their own particular alternative.

Acknowledgements

We wish to thank Professor Denis O'Brien and Mr John Ashworth for many helpful conversations and comments on earlier drafts of sections of this book. They, however, can bear no responsibility for the finished product; for that, and any errors of omission or commission, we alone are responsible.

We also wish to thank Edward Elgar who encouraged us to write this book, and for his patience when the manuscript deadline became a little flexible! Also, our thanks are due to Katy Thomas who copied and collated the whole of the final manuscript.

Finally, we must express our deep gratitude to our partners who have offered support and encouragement when needed, and for being so understanding when wordprocessing might have appeared to have been a more attractive option than their company.

Adrian C. Darnell and J. Lynne Evans,
The University of Durham

Introduction

Research in the methodology of economics is a branch of enquiry which has a long history[1] and it is an area which has attracted much interest over recent years;[2] some of the current interest in the methodology of economics may have been prompted by a spate of publications which are critical of the subject's standing and which display a dissatisfaction with the perceived accomplishments of economics.[3]

There are no universally accepted definitions of methodology, but in this text we will concentrate on that part of the enquiry which focuses upon the concepts, theories and procedures adopted by economists. The methodology of econometrics is a sub-part of the methodology of economics[4] and concerns, in particular, the procedures adopted in the testing and, where applicable, the quantification of economic theories. Within this definition of methodology we do not, therefore, include the technical procedures of economic and econometric theory.[5]

The main focus of this book is the methodology (not the technology) of econometrics. Part I contains reviews of the underlying probability concepts, the philosophy of induction, falsification and verification and the 'rise and fall' of economic positivism. In Part II the attempts of many contemporary econometricians to explain and justify their particular 'methodologies'[6] are critically examined. In these chapters the various 'econometric methodologies' of Leamer, Sims and Hendry and the 'co-integrators' will be discussed in detail, as will what is loosely labelled the 'traditional approach'.

By focusing upon these particular 'econometric methodologies' we are, essentially, concentrating upon the analysis of time-series data; however, our coverage of time-series econometrics is not intended to be, nor is it, comprehensive. It has not been able, within the scope of this book, to address the various schools of thought on cross-section analysis but it should be noted that the general prescriptions offered within our attempt to rehabilitate 'traditional econometric modelling' are equally valid, whatever the source of the data – time-series or cross-section.

Econometrics is a relatively young subject; although it is possible to find examples of very early econometric work in the last century, the Econometric Society was only formed in 1930 but the acceleration in econometric studies is largely a post-Second World War phenomenon.[7] As a cause, a consequence, or both, this period of intense activity was also marked by the rise in the availability of high speed computers, the commensurate increase in the availability of suitable software and the increasing availability of economic data. Allied to this 'improving environment' was the increasing awareness amongst economists of the work of philosophers of science, and especially the work of Sir Karl Popper.[8] Indeed, the 'methodology of econometrics' is perhaps easiest understood and approached through the perspective of the sophisticated falsificationism of Popperian methodology.

We do not align ourselves with the view of DeMarchi and Gilbert (1989) that:

> Methodology is, as everyone knows, a subject of formally acknowledged importance but carrying no weight. It is ignored by all but the young, the spent and the discontent. Partly this is because methodologists, like philosophers, are rarely practitioners, yet practitioners have a sneaky feeling that methodologists would like to tell them how they should be behaving. In fact methodology is inquiry into why the accepted is judged acceptable. (p. 9)[9]

The methodology of economics *is* of importance, therefore it has weight: it provides criteria by which to judge the efforts of economists; methodological pluralism, as would appear to be expressed by DeMarchi and Gilbert, is little different from methodological anarchy. Without 'rules' or 'norms' of behaviour, anything goes!

Econometrics is a tool which economists have at their disposal: it provides *inter alia* tests of theories and can be used to indicate which competing economic hypotheses are deserving of the greatest (current) claim to being 'maintained'.[10] Without economics, econometrics simply becomes 'metrics', though even then it would rely on some theoretical language to define the measured variables of interest; this view, therefore, denies that of De Marchi and Gilbert that:

> Econometrics is now a fully fledged and distinct discipline, lying between mathematical statistics and economics, drawing on the one and indispensable to the other (p. 11).

Methodological views of economics, simply applied, have much to say regarding the 'methodology of econometrics'; however, econometrics does not so much require its own methodology but, rather, requires direct examination within the wider context of the study of economics.

While it is relatively easy to find primary and secondary sources which provide discussions of the methodological approaches to economics in general,[11] it is not common to find an explicit consideration of the methodological status of econometric investigations.[12] But econometrics is that branch of our subject which explicitly unites deduction, induction and statistical inference and it is mainly for this reason that a discussion of the 'methodology of econometrics' is necessary.

Notwithstanding this, we do *not* attempt to discuss the methodology of economics in general; rather we wish to draw only on those aspects of that methodology which are pertinent to empirical investigations. In so doing we make no great claims to originality, but merely attempt to impose some pre-existing methodological norms on applied econometrics.

NOTES

1. See, for example, Mill (1836), Mill (1843), Cairnes (1875), Keynes (1891), Robbins (1932), Hutchison (1938), Popper (1934). See also Blaug (1980) and especially Part II: 'The history of economic methodology'.
2. See, for example, the plethora of recent texts: Blaug (1980), Boland (1982), Caldwell (1982), Dyke (1981), Hahn and Hollis (1979), Hausman (1981 and 1984), Hollis and Nell (1975), Hutchison (1977, 1978 and 1981), Katouzian (1980), Latsis (1976), Machlup (1978), Marr and Raj (1983), Pitt (1981), Rosenberg (1976), Stegmueller et al. (1982) and Stewart (1979).
3. See, for example, Bell and Kristol (1981), Eichner (1983), Leontief (1971), Phelps Brown (1972), Ward (1972), Wiles and Routh (1984) and Worswick (1972).
4. This follows from our view that econometrics is a part of the discipline of economics, rather than a discipline in its own right. There are econometricians who view econometrics as a subject distinct from economics, but we do not share this approach.
5. Thus we are not concerned with an examination of the various uses of verbal, algebraic or diagrammatic analytical methods, nor with the technical derivation of the formal techniques of econometrics. Methodology is sometimes used as a synonym for such 'technology' but in this sense methodology is merely a more striking word than 'methods' and this usage is not adopted within this book. Indeed, we are critical of those authors who use the word in this way.
6. Pagan (1987) uses the term methodology in this sense: 'Since 1975 we have seen a concerted attempt by a number of authors to build methodologies for econometric analysis.' (p. 4) However, while those who have attempted to 'build econometric methodologies' have certainly developed new batteries of techniques, and have paid some lip-service to 'Methodology' (with a capital M), we are not convinced that the work discussed by Pagan in terms of 'methodology' is actually deserving of that title.
7. There had been an abortive attempt to form an econometric society by Fisher as early as 1912 but there were too few economists interested in such a venture; see Christ (1952). For histories of econometric thought see, for example, Darnell (1984), Christ (1985), Epstein (1987) and Morgan (1989).
8. Popper's *The Logic of Scientific Discovery* was written in German and first published

in 1934; its importance was first recognized, amongst English speaking economists, by Hutchison (1938). Popper's influence on economists has been profound (see Chapter 3 for more details of this), and although his work provides a source of contact between economic methodology and the philosophy of science, much of the work in economic methodology has been written largely in ignorance of the main body of literature in that field. Hausman (1984) observed that the current 'renewed interest in economic methodology comes after decades during which the subject was largely ignored by philosophers, while the efforts of economists – in many cases prominent ones – were sporadic and often as polemical as they were philosophical. Much of the current work on the methodology of economics is unsure of itself and uninformed about the history of philosophical discussions' (p. 3). Our text is, we hope, not uninformed regarding that history, but makes no attempt to offer the reader an introduction to it either.

9. This is a most curious remark and was surely written tongue-in-cheek.
10. This is not the same as the greatest current claim to being 'true'.
11. See, for example, the work of Popper (1968), Lakatos (1978), Kuhn (1970), Laudan (1977) and the primary and secondary references given in notes 1 and 2.
12. But see chapters 7, 8 and 9 of Stewart (1979) in which there is an explicit discussion.

PART I

1. Economics, Data and Probability

Economic data may be used as a tool to facilitate one, or several, of various ends:

- to provide a quantitative calculus, that is it may be used to provide numerical measures of theoretical parameters;
- to provide a test of economic theory through a falsificationist approach;
- to attempt verification of economic theory;
- to provide a quantitative description of economic phenomena;
- as an exploratory device to prompt hypothesis formation.

These categories are not intended to be either mutually exclusive or exhaustive.[1]

Much applied econometric work is intended to provide both a test of economic theory and a quantitative calculus; examples abound.[2] However, within the voluminous literature on the methodology of economics much energy has been devoted to discussing and identifying the role of empirical analysis,[3] but very little energy has been devoted to examining the methodology of econometrics *per se*; that is, the methodological, as opposed to technological, routes by which econometricians seek to achieve their aims has been the subject of little analysis. This is not an ideal situation because the methodology implicit in the statistical model adopted by econometricians is that which was first developed by applied workers in the natural sciences[4] and the question of the applicability of statistical inferential techniques to economics is, therefore, important. It is a question which should neither be ignored nor seen as trivial. Moreover, the general philosophy of science, within which empirical analysis is embedded and which is adopted by many as the philosophical basis of economics, is also 'borrowed' from the natural sciences. As Mayo (1981) remarked: 'As with other scientists who applied statistics to their fields, workers in economics were more concerned with applying and absorbing statistical techniques into their science than with the foundational and philosophical questions associated with these methods' (pp. 175 and 176).

A primary purpose of this chapter is to discuss the probabilistic foundations of econometrics.

3

REPEATABILITY, EXPERIMENTS AND THE NATURAL AND SOCIAL SCIENCES

One of the most popular and common techniques of data analysis amongst economists is the method of ordinary least squares regression analysis. One of the earliest recorded instances of the method of least squares fitting was that of astronomers who, having made several measures of the position of a heavenly body (assumed fixed) wished to compute the 'best estimate' of that body's position. The arithmetic average of the observations is the least squares solution and, assuming that the source of variability lies only in unsystematic errors of measurement, the mean value provides the 'best linear unbiased estimator' of the true parameter (which in this case is the position of the star).[5] In such a world, the 'experiment' of measuring the position could be repeated *ad nauseam*. Such an example, in which the 'experiment' is capable, at least in principle, of being repeated, is typical of the natural sciences. More will be said below of the ability to repeat any experiment. However, social scientists rarely, if ever, are in a position to repeat any experiment; we typically take the data as given and, in many applications, are not even in a position to isolate the phenomenon under consideration from the general economic environment.[6]

One can, in fact, argue that the distinction often drawn between social and natural scientists – that the latter can experiment while the former cannot – is an illusory difference. The typical stylized experiment involves the control of 'disturbing influences' and the measurement of an outcome; this experiment is then repeated with similar control exercised and a new measurement is taken. The new measurement is expected to differ from the first; this process is then repeated until the investigator has sufficient observations for the purpose at hand.

It is not trivial to ask why the measures of the various outcomes are different. One reason might be that the measuring device (a combination, almost certainly, of a physical apparatus and a human observer) is itself subject to some kind of error: the 'true' outcomes may in fact be identical, but this cannot be observed to be the case since there are measurement errors. An alternative, though not mutually exclusive, reason might be that the control has been improperly exercised and that the material outcomes do in fact differ as a consequence.[7] It is to be noted that only a statement of faith can distinguish between these alternatives; however, since it is extraordinarily difficult to erect convincing arguments either that the measuring device is perfect or that perfect control has been exercised in any investigation (whether within the natural or social sciences), we will take the perceived difference in outcomes to be the result of the combination of both imperfect measurement and imperfect control. The weights to be attached to the two sources of difference will be specific to the investigation, and it is likely that in contrasting the natural and the social sciences the greater weight would be attached to measurement error in the former, while the greater weight would be attached to imperfect control in the latter.

The above leads us to conclude that the 'distinction' between the natural and the social scientist regarding their respective abilities to repeat experiments is one of degree, and not one of substance. Just as it may be asserted that the natural scientist cannot repeat an experiment identical in all circumstances, so may it be asserted that this possibility is denied to the social scientist.[8]

As a simple example, consider the 'repeated experiment' of rolling a dice. The measurement device consists of our observing which face of the dice lies uppermost after it has stopped rolling. Six outcomes are possible.[9] The measurement device may be asserted to be faultless, yet were we to carry out the experiment of rolling a given dice, say, ten times we would not observe the same outcome on all occasions. Why not? To answer this question it is necessary to address the question of what constitutes the 'disturbing influences' in the experiment. Amongst the obvious sources are the force with which the dice is rolled and its position immediately before being released. Other disturbing influences include the humidity and air flow around the dice and the (almost certainly) non-homogeneous surface upon which it lands and rolls. Additionally, the logical possibility that the act of rolling the dice materially alters it should be recognized.[10] Indeed, were all the disturbing influences to be identified and controlled perfectly then it may be asserted, somewhat tautologically, that the outcomes would all be identical! Equally, were all the disturbing influences to be identified it would be possible, given knowledge of all the relevant initial conditions, to say with absolute confidence what the outcome would be.[11] We do not, however, know what all the disturbing influences are, but there is widespread intersubjective agreement that the factors which determine the outcomes are both non-systematic and unpredictable. For this reason the dice rolling experiment is used in games of chance precisely because it is seen as providing a uniform random number generator.

RANDOM VARIABLES

What is meant by a random number? A random number is best understood first as a theoretical, mathematical construct; then we may attempt to identify a protocol, material, counterpart.

A random experiment R has the following characteristics:

1. The experiment is capable of being repeated indefinitely under essentially the same conditions.
2. Although it is not, in general, possible to state what a *particular* outcome will be, it is possible to describe the set of *all possible* outcomes of the experiment.
3. As the experiment is performed repeatedly, the individual outcomes seem to occur in a haphazard manner. However, as the experiment is repeated a large number of times, a definite pattern or regularity appears. It is this regularity which makes it possible to construct a precise mathematical model with which to analyse the experiment.[12]

With each experiment, R, there is a *sample space*, S, which is the set of all possible outcomes of R.[13] A function f, assigning to every element s of S a real number f(s), is a *random variable.*

Thus, in the dice-rolling experiment, the conditions are agreed by most commentators to satisfy the requirements of a random experiment, and the value of the outcome (i.e. the number of dots on the uppermost face of the dice) may be immediately interpreted as a random variable. However, one of the difficulties in recognizing a random experiment, as described above, is in knowing when the experiment in question has been repeated under *essentially the same conditions.* What are these conditions, and when may we be assured that there has been no material change from one trial to another? In order for there to be a sample space consisting of more than one element, at least one condition of the experiment must have been different, one trial to another.[14]

Indeed, if one adopts the position of a determinist[15] then to generate a sample space of more than one member requires that in repeating the trials of the experiment at least one of the salient (determining) conditions varies as the trials are repeated. On the other hand, a non-determinist[16] would argue that there exist some phenomena which are not wholly determined by material conditions, and that, even were all the initial conditions held constant,[17] the outcomes would vary across the trials because of the intrinsically *stochastic* nature of the process.

To complete the picture of a random experiment, we need now to add the notion of *probability*.

PROBABILITY

There are many interpretations of the word 'probability'.[18] Whatever approach is adopted, probabilities obey certain rules; what differs, one approach to another, is the interpretation put upon probability. Probability, whatever is meant by that term, is the foundation of statistics; however, those foundations are controversial. The main debate concerns the distinction between the so-called *Bayesian* approach and the *sampling theory* approach, but there are also subdivisions within each category which are of importance. At one level the distinction is that between *objective* and *subjective* concepts of probability, and for our present purposes this will suffice.

From a strictly mathematical viewpoint, probability is a set function satisfying certain axioms; the axioms are not debatable, but their interpretation, and the interpretation of manipulations of them, depend on the particular understanding of probability held. Let U be a universal, or reference set; a function P which assigns to every subset A of U a real number $P(A)$ is a *probability measure* on U provided that:

1. For every subset A of U, $P(A) \geq 0$.
2. $P(U) = 1$.
3. If A and B are any two *disjoint* subsets of U, and their union is denoted by C, then $P(C) = P(A) + P(B)$. (This is the axiom of 'additivity'.)

These three axioms form no bone of contention, but objectivists and subjectivists hold quite distinct views about the interpretation of the word 'probability'.

OBJECTIVE PROBABILITY

The views of objectivists are best explained by reference to the idea of a repeated experiment, described above; indeed, many of the ideas, as originally formulated, had their basis in games of chance and gambling. The first probability calculations are usually attributed to Cardano.[19] Consider the simple experiment of rolling a 'fair' dice, and suppose that the (subjective) judgement has been made that attention shall be confined to the six possible outcomes. To an objectivist, such as Cardano, the 'probability' of any one outcome is 1/6, and the reasoning is as follows: since each outcome is equally likely, the 'probability' of any one outcome is simply the ratio of the number of times that outcome can occur to the total number of possible outcomes. De Moivre, in 1718, and later Laplace, adopted this statement as a definition,[20] and it has become known as the classical definition of probability. There is, however, a serious objection to this definition: if by 'equally likely' is meant 'equally probable' then there would appear to be a presupposition of a definition of probability in defining probability.

No doubt behind this simple conception was a 'frequentist' interpretation. If the number of trials is denoted by n, and the number of occurrences of A is denoted by m then the frequentist concept of probability is that the probability of A, $P(A)$, is given by the ratio m/n. Of course, as the number of trials changes, so will the ratio m/n, and to avoid the undesirable result that the probability measure depend on the number of trials, the frequency definition of probability is as follows:

$$P(A) = \lim_{n \to \infty} (m/n)$$

Thus probability is defined as the limit of a relative frequency; however, this definition requires that the limit exists, and of course we cannot form a conclusive test of its existence.[21] As an example, let A be the event that the dice lands with its uppermost face reading a six; then if in 100 trials there are observed to be 18 occurrences of this event, the probability would be given by 18/100 or 0.18; in 1000 trials the ratio might be 0.17; the frequency definition is the limit of such ratios, but this limit cannot be observed materially. Many experiments exist, like the dice-rolling experiment or a coin-tossing experiment, in which there is intersubjective agreement that the 'long-run' frequency does converge to a limit,[22] but this can only be interpreted as a *subjective judgement*. This definition, using the limit of a relative frequency, is due to Poisson and was published in his *Recherches sur la Probabilité des Jugements* in 1837.[23] In an experimental world in which there is intersubjective agreement that the experiment has, indeed, been repeated with all essential conditions held constant, the classical definition and the frequentist definition will coincide and are, no doubt, adequate for many purposes.

However, the social scientist (among others) deals with non-experimental data in a non-standardized, and non-standardizable, environment. To approach the concept of probability in a non-repeatable environment, consider first the many 'probability type' statements made in everyday language: the 'chance' of rain tomorrow, the 'chance' of a particular horse winning a particular race, the 'chance' of Labour winning the next election, etc. Neither the classical approach nor the frequentist approach can provide non-trivial answers to such questions: the named events will either occur or they will not and there is no possibility of repeating the trial.[24] A frequency may only be identified within the context of a well defined class of repeated trials of an experiment, and no such class exists in the examples given. To the objectivist, the answer to the question 'What is the chance of rain tomorrow?' is either one (if it rains) or zero (otherwise). A somewhat related issue is that frequencies are identified with respect to classes of events, not to a particular event. We may say that a 'fair dice' will exhibit a probability of 1/6 of showing a six, but what does this say about the outcome of any one individual roll of the dice?[25]

On the question of the probability of an individual event (whether as part of a repeated experimental framework or not), three distinct responses are possible:[26]

1. Probabilities are only defined for stochastic events which have not occurred; probability does not apply to historical 'facts'.
2. Probabilities do not apply to individual events, but only to classes of events.
3. Probabilities are defined for individual events, past and future, under specific conditions.

The first view requires the timing of the event to be known and thus, adopting this position, ' probability' is defined with reference to a specific information set containing, among other things, statements of the precise timing of the event under consideration.[27] The second view effectively denies the application of probability to individual events, and the final view asserts that meaningful probability statements can only be made about some individual events. The circumstance under which this is possible requires that *there are no recognizable subsets within the class.*[28] Most classical inferential procedures seem to adopt either the first or the second interpretation. Of the many possible reasons for this position, one of the more important is that the third view makes demands on the investigator's personal information set: information regarding the presence or otherwise of recognizable subsets is required and this demands a personal definition of probability. However, the first interpretation makes similar demands, and thus, to make any meaningful statements about the 'probability' of a *single* event, objective probability has limited applicability: it is only meaningful to speak of the objective probability of a 'random' event which, it is agreed, has not yet occurred. As is well known, social scientists often wish to make probability-type statements regarding single events and, especially, often wish to quantify ignorance regarding events which are essentially non-stochastic (such as the quantification of our ignorance regarding the size of a theoretical parameter which is deemed to be fixed). The quantification of ignorance is made through the language of probability, and consequently, as Hicks (1979) observed: 'Probability, in economics, must mean something wider [than objective probability]' (p. 107).

SUBJECTIVE PROBABILITY

The view that probability is not a physical but a personal concept was first put forward by James Bernoulli in *Ars Conjectandi* (1713), in which he suggested that probability is a 'degree of confidence' which an *individual* associates with an uncertain event; clearly this conception of probability will vary from one individual to another, with regard both to which events are 'uncertain' and to the degree of confidence held. This conceptualization of probability, therefore, places great weight on the individual's personal information set: when an individual lacks perfect knowledge regarding an event, that event will be identified as uncertain, whereas to an individual who holds perfect knowledge that same event will be deemed certain. Similarly, for events deemed by any two individuals to be uncertain, the 'degree of confidence' will be determined by the personal information available to each individual. As an example of this, consider the question 'how probable is it that Gladstone was the twentieth Prime Minister of Great Britain?' The response from an individual who *knows* whether or not Gladstone was indeed the twentieth Prime Minister is either one or zero, but the response from an individual who lacks this perfect knowledge will be some fraction (possibly expressed in the form of 'betting odds').

To take an example from classical statistics, and one often encountered in economics, consider the construction and interpretation of a confidence interval. If a sample of size n is taken at random from a population which is assumed to have a normal distribution with unknown mean θ and known variance σ^2 then the 95 per cent interval is given by the formula:

$$\bar{x} \pm 1.96 \, (\sigma/\sqrt{n})$$

Now suppose that from a particular sample, this interval formula leads to the computation of a lower limit of 2 and an upper limit of 5. The interpretation of the interval *formula* (as opposed to the particular interval constructed from the one sample) is that the probability of the interval containing the true, but unknown, parameter θ is 0.95. (Note that in this interpretation it is the interval, not the parameter, which is the random variable.) On a frequentist interpretation, were the formula to be applied to each and every possible sample drawn randomly from the population, then 95 per cent of all intervals so constructed would contain the true parameter while 5 per cent would not. Both interpretations apply to a class of events which has not occurred (views 1 and 2 above); the actual observation of a realization of the interval of (2, 5) is an individual event; neither 2 nor 5 is a random number and, equally, θ is not random. Since we have no random numbers *after* the drawing of the sample the particular interval so constructed either contains the unknown parameter or it does not; what probability interpretation may then be made? In the absence of any recognizable subsets, the response might be that the relevant probability is 0.95, but this probability statement is being made *a posteriori,* not *a priori*; *a priori* objective probability may be applied to such an individual event, but *a posteriori* there are no random variables in the statement, and so to what does the probability apply? One answer would, therefore, appear to be that no objective probability statement applies *after the event* but one can, nevertheless, make intelligent statements using subjective probability.[29] However, before examining what *can* be said in this context, an important question regarding subjective probability must be posed: in what sense are subjective probabilities (or degrees of belief) interpretable as probabilities and how, if at all, are degrees of belief measurable?

One may take the view that all events (whether historical or otherwise) have, as an inherent property, a 'degree of belief' attached to them by all individuals.[30] Such a view is a consequence of asserting, as an axiom, that given a body of knowledge (what has been referred to above as an information set) and two uncertain events A and B, then either A is deemed more likely than B, or vice versa, or A and B are deemed equally likely. This does not require any specific measurement of 'likelihood', but merely the ordering of the 'likelihood' of the events.[31] From this ranking, it is then reasonable to ask under what conditions this leads to a probability measure, P, such that $P(A) > P(B)$ if and only if A is deemed more likely than B. Of the conditions necessary, the first is that the ranking order is transitive, that is if A_1 is more likely than A_2, and A_2 is more likely than A_3, and . . . . and A_{n-1} is more likely than A_n, then A_1 is more likely than A_n; the second requirement is that of additivity (this is property 3, p. 7).[32]

Another approach is that of Ramsey (1926) who examined subjective probability in the context of decision making under uncertainty: probability is then defined in circumstances where an individual has to make a decision and future states of the world, and hence the rewards, are uncertain. Yet another approach is that of deFinetti (1937) who examined the relationship between betting odds and probability. This approach proceeds from the *coherence principle* which states that no party to a wager will proceed if a sure loss will be made. This simple axiom may be shown to be capable of generating the three axioms of probability given above. However, two objections have been made to this demonstration: first the two sides to the wager may hold different information and, second, the decision whether or not to wager may be contingent on the size of the stakes. Both objections have some validity, and it may be concluded that it is a little unwise to define probabilities in the context of any specific decision theoretic problem.

So are degrees of belief probabilities? At one level this may be answered by saying that there are compelling intuitive reasons for viewing measures of uncertain knowledge as probabilities (that is, constraining degrees of belief to conform to the axiomatic basis of a probability measure), and at another level we may suggest that a 'rational' decision maker will behave as if their degrees of belief were held according to the axioms of probability.[33] While the first response has some appeal, albeit by reference to the notion of intuition, the second response has deficiencies since it defines probability and rationality in circular fashion.

Objective probability statements arise from a world in which it is asserted that material measurement of uncertainty is possible; however, this typically denies the attachment of probability to events which have occurred, and always denies the attachment of probability to events which are not random. Subjective probability has its origin in a ranking of events by reference to an individual's assessment of their likelihood. If that subjective view is then translated into a numerical measure which obeys the axiomatic statement of what constitutes a 'probability measure' those degrees of belief are transformed into real numbers, lying in the closed interval [0, 1]. Essentially, then, subjective degrees of belief, however stated, originate in a ranking but are, nevertheless, capable of a cardinal interpretation; objective probability, although it might appear to have a relationship with a material counterpart in an experimental framework, relies on either a circular argument[34] or must make recourse to an inductive conclusion. The use of a subjective interpretation of probability has the advantage that it allows single events, in a non-repeatable environment, to be described according to their 'chance' of occurrence; in the attempt to quantify and reduce ignorance of social phenomena economists must call on an ability to describe and communicate uncertainty in a non-repeatable environment. As Hicks (1979) remarked: 'The probabilities of "states of the world" that are formally used by economists . . cannot be interpreted in terms of random experiments. Probability, in economics, must mean something wider' (p. 107).

The use of subjective probability, allied to Bayes's Rule,[35] provides the basis of Bayesian statistics; the rule offers a theory of learning, for it provides a method of combining 'prior probabilities' with data information (the likelihood) to form the 'posterior probabilities'. Inference proceeds, then, from the posterior probabilities.[36] In this text a wholeheartedly Bayesian approach is not adopted, but the interpretation of probability models is based on a subjective, degrees of belief, concept of probability.

PROBABILITY AND ECONOMIC DATA

The relationship of the above discussion to economic data and to inferential practice amongst economists is best seen as a cautionary tale. Many users of data proceed on the basis of a statistical model, erected on a foundation of probability, and never ask (nor sometimes even recognize) the important questions regarding the applicability of that model to the particular circumstances of their investigations.[37] Economists, and other social scientists, deal almost exclusively with data generated outside the context of an experiment (let alone an experiment which they have designed and for which they are responsible). The conditions of the world within which our data are generated are outside the control of the investigator; the possibility of repeating the conditions does not exist (typically), yet the model of inference adopted by economists is largely classical in both exposition and interpretation. The classical model, with its attendant repeated experimental foundations, is strictly inapplicable to economic data which have not been collected through sampling. However, the rest of this section will provide a justification of the use of classical distributional theory within the context of non-experimental data, treating the observed economic variables *as if they were the result* of a single drawing from a population. This judgement is based on an interpretation of probability as a degree of belief.

The classical regression model and its associated least squares estimation method, as used by economists, utilizes the assumption that the so-called 'error term' has certain properties 'in repeated sampling'. The economist is denied the possibility of sampling repeatedly, but can we proceed as if the data were the result of a single drawing from a random experiment? Consider the following stylized framework of analysis.

Let Y denote a theoretical variable of interest; and let X denote a vector (perhaps of infinite dimension) of theoretical variables; let Y^* and X^* denote their respective observable material proxies (i.e. the actual measures of the proxy variables). Let Y^{**} denote the 'true' (but unobservable) value of the proxy variable Y^* and X^{**} the 'true' (but unobservable) value of the proxy variables X^*.

We may then posit the existence of an exact relationship between Y and X;[38] let this be of the general form $Y = F(X)$.[39]

This may also be written as:

$$Y = f(X_1 . . X_n) + [F(X) - f(X_1 . . X_n)]$$

In this expression we have focused on the relationship between Y and the first n components of X (using an assumed functional form, f), and the rest is a remainder. This may be further decomposed if we assume that the function F is separable. Thus if we suppose that:

$$F(X) = F_1(X_1 . . X_n) + F_2(X_{n+1} . . X_N)$$

(where N need not be finite), then:

$$Y = f(X_1 . . X_n)$$
$$+[F_1(X_1 . . X_n) - f(X_1 . . X_n)]$$
$$+F_2(X_{n+1} . . X_N)$$

Then we may write the relationship as:

$$Y = f(X_1 . . X_n) + e$$

where the discrepancy, e, is defined by:

$$e = [F_1(X_1 \ldots X_n) - f(X_1 \ldots X_n)]$$
$$+ F_2(X_{n+1} \ldots X_N)$$

However, the Y and X variables are not observable: they are theoretical variables; what are observed are the Y^* and X^* values, but these variables are themselves (possibly imperfect) measures of the chosen material counterparts of Y and X.

Now suppose that the measured proxy Y^* and the 'unobservable protocol counterpart' Y^{**} are related by $Y^* = Y^{**} + m_o$ (W) where W denotes a vector of variables which determine the measurement discrepancy between Y^* and Y^{**}. Further, suppose that the theoretical variable Y is related to its unobservable protocol counterpart by

$$Y = Y^{**} + p_Y$$

where p_Y is the error encapsulating the lack of exact correspondence between the theoretical and protocol variables. Then:

$$Y = Y^* - m_o(W) + p_Y$$

and

$$Y^* = f(X_1 \ldots X_n) + v \text{ where}$$
$$v = e + m_o(W) - p_Y, \text{ i.e.}$$
$$v = [F_1(X_1 \ldots X_n) - f(X_1 \ldots X_n)]$$
$$+ F_2(X_{n+1} \ldots X_N) + m_o(W) - p_Y$$

However, the X variables are not observable either; what we observe are the measurable protocol counterparts X^*, and hence we write the relationship between measurable variables as:

$$Y^* = f(X_1^* \ldots X_n^*) + u$$

where the discrepancy, u, is given by:

$$u = f(X_1 \ldots X_n) - f(X_1^* \ldots X_n^*) + v, \text{ i.e.}$$
$$u = [f(X_1 \ldots X_n) - f(X_1^* \ldots X_n^*)]$$
$$+ [F_1(X_1 \ldots X_n) - f(X_1 \ldots X_n)]$$
$$+ F_2(X_{n+1} \ldots X_N)$$

$$+ m_o(W)$$
$$-p_Y$$

This error comprises five distinct components:

1. The first square bracketed term is due to the measurement and proxy errors in the first n variables of X.
2. The second square bracketed term is due to the assumed functional form in f, which may not be identical to the true functional form F_1.
3. The third term is due to the omitted theoretical variables $X_{n+1} .. X_N$.
4. The fourth term is due to the measurement error between the unobservable protocol variable Y^{**} and its measure Y^*.
5. The fifth term is due to the proxy error between the theoretical variable Y and its unobservable protocol counterpart, Y^{**}.

Putting this in the context of economic theory and method, we identify the component f$(X_1^* .. X_n^*)$ as comprising a statement of economic theory in which the salient determinants of the dependent variable are identified as the first n variables of the vector X, the chosen measures are given by $(X_1^* .. X_n^*)$, the dependent variable is measured by Y^* and the functional form relating the regressand and the regressors is chosen as f. Theory would, typically, predict the signs of at least all the first partial derivatives of f; moreover, the predictions of theory (i.e. the signs of the responses of the dependent variable to its determinants) may be viewed as the *composite main hypothesis* of interest. However, a main hypothesis cannot be examined without imposing some assumptions, otherwise known as *tentative auxiliary hypotheses*. These auxiliary hypotheses include, *inter alia*:

- The salient variables are the first n components of X and are measured by the observable vector X^*.
- The influence of these chosen determinants may be captured through the functional form f.
- The errors and omissions in this simple representation, encapsulated in the discrepancy term u, form a *non-systematic influence*.

The operational sense of a non-systematic influence requires some explanation. Specifically, we require that the term u has the following characteristics:

(a)　For any given set of observations on the chosen determinants, the probability that u lies in any arbitrary interval (a, b) is identical to the probability that u lies in the interval $(-a, -b)$. As a consequence, u is as likely to be positive as negative, is symmetric about its median (which is zero) and has a zero mean.

(b)　For any two given sets of observations on the chosen determinants, the probability that the discrepancy associated with the first set lies in the arbitrary interval (a, b) is identical to the probability that the discrepancy associated with the second set lies in the interval (a, b).

(c)　The conditional probability of u lying in any arbitrary interval, given knowledge of the observed values $(X_1^* .. X_n^*)$, is identical to the probability of u lying in that interval, i.e. u and the chosen, measurable, salient determinants of Y^* are independent of each other.

(d)　The conditional probability that the discrepancy, u, associated with a particular set of observed determinants lies in any arbitrary interval, given knowledge of the actual discrepancies associated with other realizations of the determinants is identical to the probability that u lies in that interval, i.e. the discrepancies are independent of each other.

The requirement that u should behave in a non-systematic fashion as defined by the conditions above may be rationalized as follows: were any one of the characteristics listed above violated, this would indicate that a systematic influence on Y^* had not been explicitly modelled through the chosen functional form f and through the chosen set of determinants $(X_1^* .. X_n^*)$. Were this the case, then the model would be deficient in an important sense, for it would have relegated at least one systematic component to the error term; this would then deny the composite assumption that the variables $(X_1^* .. X_n^*)$ and their associated functional form, f, represent *the* influence of 'salient' determinants since, in this case, either that set is but a *subset* of the salient determinants or the chosen functional form is deficient (or both).

Thus we have identified those characteristics of the 'errors, omissions and approximations' (i.e. the auxiliary hypotheses) which, in conjunction with the main (composite) hypothesis, allow the main hypothesis to be examined.

THE INTERPRETATION OF THE ERROR AS A WHITE NOISE TERM

Such 'errors, omissions and approximations' which form the discrepancy could, under these conditions, be modelled as a *white noise random variable*. It is important to note that this device does not require us to believe (or assert) that the economic phenomenon under consideration is actually the outcome of some random experiment; rather the framework of analysis, in which the non-systematic component is required to have certain very specific characteristics, allows us to view the behaviour of the error term u, as analogous to a white noise process.

Specifically, our ignorance of the full set of determinants (i.e. our ignorance of the vector X which may or may not be finite) and the approximations implicit in identifying a subset of X as salient variables, in identifying a particular functional form f and in using measured variables which may be both imperfect measures and imperfect proxies of our theoretical constructs, are all encapsulated in the term u which describes only the non-systematic influences on the dependent variable.

Thus we do not assert that any experiment has actually taken place, nor do we assert that the observed data are the result of any stylized drawing from a random experiment; equally we do not assert that the 'errors, omissions and approximations' constitute a protocol random variable. What has been offered above is a formalization of the rationale for our adopting the concept of a random variable, especially in the form of a white noise variable, which is a precise representation of the non-systematic component of a formal statement of economic theory. The probability concepts implicit in this representation are, therefore, not those of the classical probabilist who adopts the model of a repeated experiment, nor those of the frequentist who, equally, requires the concept of a repeated number of trials. Rather, the model used is one of *as if* methodology in which we assert, as a testable tentative hypothesis, that our data may, for our purposes, be modelled as if they were the observed outcome of drawing a random sample from a population. Randomness is a metaphor – it is the chosen way of modelling ignorance. The ignorance arises with respect to the material relationships between economic variables and it is the object of economic inquiry to reduce that area of ignorance – to be able to quote shorter odds on specific events.

In requiring that the non-systematic component of a well specified equation behaves as if it were a drawing from a random distribution there is no effective, material, counterpart of a repeated experiment on which we may call; we may, however, state that the sought-after properties of the error term imply that it may be modelled as if it were a random variable. This allows the properties (*a*) – (*d*) above to be written in probability language: *u* may be treated as if it were a random variable with probability density function g(*u*) such that:

(a′) Denoting by u_i the error associated with the *i*th set of observations (denoted by X^i), g(u_i) is a symmetric function about zero. Specifically, this implies that E(u_i) = 0 for all *i*.

(b′) The conditional probability of u_i given X^i is identical to the conditional probability of u_j given X^j, i.e. the conditional density functions of u_i and u_j are identical for all *i* and *j*. Specifically, this implies that all the errors have conditional distributions which have a common variance.

(c′) The conditional probability of u_i given X^i is the probability density function g(u_i); i.e. u_i and its associated regressors, X^i are independent.

(d′) The conditional distribution of u_i given other errors u_j (*j* not equal to *i*) is the probability density function g(u_i); i.e. u_i is independent of the other errors, and this holds for all *i*.

The probability concept used is not an objective concept having its foundation in a repeated experimental environment; it is more a subjective concept – the investigator holds degrees of belief in the role of the 'errors, omissions and approximations' in the modelling process which forms the probabilistic basis of statistical inference. This particular approach does, of course, require some modifications to the classical interpretations of inference so common amongst economists.

One immediate modification arises in interpreting the simple regression model written, typically, as:

$$Y = X\beta + u$$

where *Y* is a vector of observations on the 'dependent variable', *X* is a matrix of observations on the 'independent variables' and *u* is a white noise error. The discussion of modelling above suggests that the regression formulation may only be seen as an initial encapsulation of the main and auxiliary hypotheses for *u* is only to be treated as if it were a white noise error *once the main and auxiliary hypotheses have been appropriately modelled*. In this interpretation, within an 'appropriate' framework of analysis there can be no 'problems' with the error term (such as heteroscedasticity or autocorrelation, failures of (*b′*) and (d′) respectively), since what is 'appropriate' is itself defined by reference to the properties of the error term u. As another example of the implications of this approach, consider an equation such as that given above which, having 'not failed' any diagnostics tests of the dichotomization into a systematic component $X\beta$ and a non-systematic white noise term u,[40] is then used to test some hypothesis of interest. Specifically, suppose that a test of the null hypothesis that some particular element of the response vector is zero is 'rejected' 'at the 5 per cent level'. A classical interpretation would be on the following lines: the null hypothesis could be true, but the sample observed would then have to be interpreted as atypical. This follows because the particular test statistic observed could only be generated, *if the null hypothesis were true,* on 5 per cent of all occasions (that is the observed result could only be generated from 5 per cent of all possible samples in a repeated sampling world). Because this is deemed to be so unlikely (i.e. the particular sample is deemed not to be atypical) the decision is to reject the null hypothesis. The proposed use of subjective probability requires very little change to this interpretation; the observed data which give rise to an 'unlikely' test statistic lead the investigator to attach a very low degree of belief to the null hypothesis which has been tested, and more especially lead to a very high degree of belief in the role of the particular variable whose influence has been examined. It should be emphasized that in order to be confident that the test statistics have their assumed distributions ('t' or 'F' for example) it is necessary to examine the nature of the error structure, and be assured that the underlying error process may indeed be treated as if it were a non-systematic, and normal, random variable. Thus, to test any main hypothesis, it is necessary to verify that the model is properly specified.

The assumed probability distribution of the error term is a formal representation of those errors, approximations and omissions which have been incurred in the process of modelling an economic theory into testable form; the concept of probability does not rely on a model of repeated experiments, but is interpreted as a reflection of 'degrees of belief'. Consequently, any computed test statistics are then used to describe degrees of belief in the hypotheses under consideration. Thus the result which leads to 'rejection at the 5 per cent level' simply says that we attach a very small degree of belief to that null hypothesis. The 'low' degree of belief is such that we would consider the 'fair' betting odds to be 19 to 1 against that hypothesis. (The longer the odds against a hypothesis, the more unlikely it is thought to be true.) The distinction is subtle: under subjective probability, the hypothesis itself is deemed to have probability attached to it whereas under the objective (classical) interpretation the probability statement is properly attached to the correctness (or otherwise) of the decision to reject. To emphasize this point, it should be remembered that under the classical interpretation, all hypotheses are either true or false – the uncertainty is attached to the decision to reject or not; under the subjective interpretation, we can attach degrees of belief to any uncertain event, including the status of tentatively held hypotheses.

That the differences between competing views of probability can, in many circumstances, be reflected only in subtle distinctions of interpretation is not to diminish the importance of any distinctions. Much criticism of statistical and econometric practice is focused on the classical framework of repeatability upon which it appears to rely.[41] The purpose of this chapter has been to discuss the probability foundations of statistical inference with non-experimental data and to suggest that, with appropriate interpretations, much of the battery of probability calculus remains available to us; however, some subtle changes of interpretation are required. Moreover, by highlighting the relationship between the 'error term' of econometrics and an economic model (a process which deliberately focuses on a chosen set of systematic components, while leaving only *non-systematic* components in the remainder), a rationale for our adopting a probabilistic calculus has been provided. This allows us to leave behind the notions of 'repeated sampling', and directs us to holding 'degrees of belief'. Naturally, their subjective nature may be the source of objection to such a procedure, but such an objection is, perhaps, more easily countered than are objections to the classical procedure (with its attendant requirement that there be a repeated experiment) which has no material counterpart.

CONCLUSION

Inferential procedures are simply a method of communicating the combination of deductive theory with observational statements;[42] the process of econometrics is, therefore, a particular blend of inferential and deductive processes. Many sceptics of data analysis are happy to adopt a nihilistic attitude simply because the methodology, as commonly expressed, utilizes a 'repeated sampling' reference which can have no material counterpart. However, it has been argued above that it is possible to use a subjective probability approach, which refers to degrees of belief in order to capture those components of a theoretical structure which are not otherwise modelled explicitly in its testable form. Within this approach, the judgement is made, initially, that it is reasonable to view the error in a regression equation as if it were the result of drawing one sample from a hypothetical population. This judgement is testable, and can lead to a reformulation of the testable form of the main hypothesis of interest.[43]

This perspective is offered in an attempt to answer those sceptics of econometrics who focus on the admitted weakness of reliance on an inapplicable 'frequentist' probabilistic foundation of econometrics; moreover, by identifying the nature of the various contributions to 'error' in a regression equation, this discussion also provides a foundation on which to erect appropriate modelling strategies.

NOTES

1. The use of data as a means of 'falsifying' or 'verifying' economic theory is largely the subject of Chapter 2. The routes by which such ends might be achieved are the subject of Chapters 4, 5, 6, 7 and 8; these chapters also discuss the role of data to achieve the other ends listed in the text.

2. See, for example, the various texts on applied econometrics, such as Bridge (1971), Rao and Miller (1971), Wallis (1973), Hebden (1983), Mayes (1981) and Thomas (1985) .

3. The discussion of the role of empirical analysis has largely been conducted in terms of the usage of data as a test of theory or as the source of hypothesis formation, and whether data should be used in an attempt to verify or falsify economic theory. The methodology of various applied econometric practices – the 'traditional approach', the approaches of Hendry, Leamer and Sims and the 'cointegration' approach – are examined in subsequent chapters of this book.

4. Econometrics has largely adopted (and in part adapted) an approach which was developed to answer questions within quite different disciplines. For histories of econometrics, see Darnell (1984), Christ (1985), Epstein (1987), Morgan (1989) and the special issue of the *Oxford Economic Papers* (1989) edited by de Marchi and Gilbert.

5. Galileo (1632) examined the question of determining the true position of a star in this way; see Darnell (1984) pp. 160–1 for details.

6. The obvious exception to this is in 'microeconometrics' where the focus of attention is on panel data. For a survey of the benefits and limitations of panel data, see Hsiao (1985) and the discussion which follows that paper.

7. This may be because some salient features of the experimental process are altered by virtue of the experiment *per se*. For example, at a somewhat naive level, consider an experiment in which a particular piece of apparatus is used repeatedly. What evidence could be deemed convincing that the experiment itself leaves the characteristics of the apparatus unchanged from one trial to another? However, experiments are designed so that it is almost certainly the case that there would be great intersubjective agreement regarding the stability of the environment within which the experiment has been repeated, and we need not be further concerned with this point, except to draw some lessons for the 'design' of the testable form of economic hypotheses.

8. However, given the greater ability of 'experimental' scientists (such as physicists) to control disturbing influences, one would expect that the outcomes arising from experiments in the natural sciences would exhibit less variability than outcomes from non-experimental social science.

9. Any one of the faces (one through six) may lie uppermost, but there is the conceptual possibility that the dice comes to rest on an edge and, strictly, there are at least twelve outcomes in this category since a dice has twelve edges; such unlikely outcomes will be ignored, but see note 13.

10. Thus a 'once rolled dice' may be materially different from a 'twice rolled dice' which may itself differ from a 'thrice rolled dice' and so on.

11. Whether such an exact forecast constitutes a 'prediction' is a moot point and more than semantics.

12. This definition is taken from Meyer (1971) pp. 7, 8.

13. The decision to identify some states of the world as outcomes of the experiment, and to exclude others, is a matter of judgement. This implies, therefore, that even in this 'objective' view of a random variable, there are subjective elements. As an illustration, it was decided in the earlier discussion to identify the sample space of the dice-rolling experiment as comprising only six outcomes, when many other outcomes (such as the dice comes to rest on an edge) are also conceivable.

14. Hicks (1979), p. 106, makes the same point. Incidentally, even if the outcomes are identical in any number of distinct trials, this does not constitute sufficient evidence from which to conclude that the initial conditions of each trial were identical; it could be, for example, that the outcome is determined by a range of factors, and between any two trials a number of them differ but in a perfectly compensating fashion.

15. A determinist is here used in the sense of one who believes that all outcomes may be wholly explained as the result of a set of non-stochastic causes, whether or not we are aware of that set.

16. A non-determinist is here used in the sense of one who believes that not all events may be wholly explained as the result of a set of non-stochastic causes, and who, therefore, believes that some events have an inherently unpredictable, stochastic (random), component.

17. That is, even if the phenomenon were observed *ceteris paribus*.

18. For a discussion of various interpretations of 'probability', see, for example, the Appendix to Swamy *et al.* (1985) pp. 48–55, or Leamer (1978) pp. 22–40.

19. Cardano was an Italian mathematician (and gambler). He wrote on the subject of the theory of games of chance, and his work was later taken up by mathematicians.

20. De Moivre published the influential *Doctrine of Chances* in 1718 and Laplace published *Théorie Analytique des Probabilités* in 1812, followed by *Essai Philosophique des Probabilités* in 1814. For discussion of the history of probability, see Todhunter (1949).

21. To assert that the limit exists is a form of an inductivist argument; see Chapter 2 for a critique of inductivism. At most the limiting ratio should be interpreted as representing a 'degree of belief' regarding the 'long-run relative frequency'.

22. The limit is that given by the objectivist approach.

23. See Todhunter *op. cit.*

24. However, if the questions are asked more generally, such as what is the probability of rain on one day of the next week, or what is the probability of a particular horse winning one of its next six outings, or what is the probability of Labour winning one of the next two General Elections, then (making assumptions of independence of trials and constant 'probabilities') these events may be viewed as Bernoulli trials and a frequentist probability may be offered.

25. The previous objection of circularity should not be overlooked in this apparently trivial example: is a 'fair dice' defined by reference to its probability structure or by

some independent property? If the latter, what is that property, and if the former, we have a circular statement.

26. See, for example, Leamer (1978) pp. 26–7.

27. This 'objective' response has 'personal, subjective' components: it relies on an information set containing statements of the timing of events, and this information may not be common property across all individuals.

28. A recognizable subset exists if its frequency is known to be different from the frequency of the complete class of events.

29. When the concept of the 'confidence interval' was first introduced by Neyman (1934) at the Royal Statistical Society, Bowley, in his vote of thanks, remarked: 'I am not sure that the "confidence interval" is not a "confidence trick" . . Does it really lead us towards what we need – the chance that in the universe we are sampling the proportion is within these certain limits? I think it does not . . The statement of the theory is not convincing, and until I am convinced I am doubtful of its validity' (p. 609 of the discussion of Neyman, 1934). For further details of this episode, see Darnell (1981) pp. 165–8.

30. What is inherent is the attachment of a 'degree of belief', not the actual quantification of that degree. This may be compared to and contrasted with the concept of physical mass. Just as a physical body has, as an inherent property, a mass, so do all events have degrees of belief associated with them; however, while the quantification of mass (within a given measurement system) is not obviously a personal judgement, the quantification of the degree of belief is dependent on the individual's own information set and the way in which that information is processed.

31. This may be seen as analogous to an ordinal utility function: individuals are assumed to hold a preference ranking over bundles of consumer goods (an ordering of the 'likelihood' of events), but are not required to be able to measure 'utility' ('probability') in a cardinal sense.

32. On a frequency definition, probability is clearly a cardinal measure; however, following Jeffreys's (1961) *Theory of Probability* (the first edition was published in 1939), it may be shown that the cardinality of subjectively held degrees of belief is a direct consequence of imposing the simple axiomatic structure given earlier in this chapter. For further details see also DeGroot (1970) .

33. It is also worth noting the distinction between two sorts of subjectivist: the *personalists* and the *necessarists*. Personalists (deFinetti, 1937; Ramsey, 1926 and Savage, 1954 for example) argue that just as knowledge is distributed across individuals, so are measures of confidence in that varying knowledge. Necessarists (Keynes, 1921; and Jeffreys, 1961 for example) argue that probability is that degree of belief which it is *rational* to hold with respect to some body of uncertain knowledge.

34. The circularity arises because one must first define 'random experiments' before one can define 'probability' and vice versa.

35. Thomas Bayes's work on 'inverse probability' was published posthumously in 1763; the Bayesian approach views parameters as random variables to capture the investigator's prior ignorance of the 'true' value and uses sample information to modify the prior judgement through the rule of conditional probability.

36 For details of Bayesian econometrics, see, for example, Zellner (1971), Box and Tiao (1973) or, at a very introductory level, Theil (1978) chapter 16.

37. Two most interesting exceptions to this are the papers by Swamy, Conway and von zur Muehlen (1985a) and by Poirier (1988a). Both papers are followed by fascinating discussions; see Boland (1985), Good (1985), Pesaran (1985), Seidenfeld (1985), Smiley (1985), and the reply by Swamy *et al.* (1985b); see also Rust (1988), Pagan (1988), Geweke (1988), and the reply by Poirier (1988b).

38. This is written without an error term; thus the relationship implicitly belongs to a non-stochastic (i.e. deterministic) framework. An error term could be added with little

consequence to the following analysis: it would merely entail the adding of another source of error to the final equation relating observable variables.

39. In this simple exposition, it is presumed that economic theory dictates only that Y is determined by the elements of X, and that no 'feedback' from Y to any X_i exists. Thus what follows is a single equation formulation. If economic theory suggests that there is dependency from X to Y and that there is also dependency from Y to at least one X_i then a simultaneous equation system is required to model that theory. As presented, the X variables are exogenous to the model (that is, the values of X are not determined within the model), and the one variable, Y, is the endogenous variable. This is, in principle, a testable assumption and it is not difficult to modify the presentation in the text to accommodate endogenous elements of the vector X, but such modifications are not presented. Modelling within a simultaneous equation framework is the particular concern of Sims, whose work is examined in Chapter 7.

40. For details of diagnostic tests, see, for example, Pesaran and Pesaran (1987) and the references cited therein. The particular use of diagnostic tests in the specification of a regression equation is discussed in some detail in Chapter 4.

41. For such criticisms see, for example, Hicks (1979), chapter VIII, and McCloskey (1985a). In the latter, the question is posed 'From what universe is a times series a random sample, and if there is one, is it one we wish to know about?' (p. 171). It is our argument that any economic data may be *conceived* as being a random sample from a hypothetical population, and that this implies certain testable properties of the data which contribute to the *design* of the framework of data analysis.

42. This is notwithstanding the fact that all observational statements are made through the 'window' of some theory. This point is expanded in Chapter 2.

43. The ways in which reformulation may take place, and the direction in which reformulation occurs, is examined in detail in Chapter 4.

2. Empirical Analysis as Scientific Explanation

Deduction and induction are both styles of reasoning used extensively in economics. They are not, however, polar positions but are intimately related to one another and both styles have, individually and jointly, exerted a marked influence on economic thought. Within the method of applied econometrics, though not necessarily within econometric theory, the two approaches are fused.

Induction is a general label which emphasizes the role of data as a major vehicle by which to accumulate knowledge and the inductive method seeks to draw general conclusions based on a finite number of particular observations. In the nineteenth century, the standard view of what constituted scientific procedure was an inductivist model: scientists begin with facts drawn from their unprejudiced observations of the real world, they then derive more general statements (universal laws) through inductive reasoning and, finally, from these laws they induce yet further generalizations, called theories. It was further believed that the truth content of both laws and theories could be adequately examined by comparing the empirical implications of those generalizations with actual observations. This view of science is that expounded, for example, by Mill in his *System of Logic, Ratiocinative and Inductive* (1843) and remains a commonly held view of the scientific method. In the latter half of the nineteenth century, however, this view of science was largely replaced. Following criticisms of the 'inductive model', the *hypothetico-deductive method* emerged early in the twentieth century.[1]

The hypothetico-deductive model of scientific explanation was formally stated in a number of works, notably those of Popper (1934), Hempel (1942) and Hempel and Oppenheim (1948). The central tenet of this approach is that all scientific explanations are characterized by their use of a common logical structure which involves an *explanans*[2] from which, using only the formal rules of logic, the *explanadum* is deduced. Within this view there is a symmetry between explanation and prediction: both use precisely the same rules of logic, but while explanation starts with a phenomenon to be explained, and proceeds to find that universal law and set of initial conditions which logically imply the event, prediction starts with a universal law and a set of initial conditions from which, through logic, a prediction about the event is derived. The essence of the hypothetico-deductive method is that it only utilizes the rules of deductive logic: the universal laws with which it begins are not derived from induction, but are hypotheses, subject to tests of their validity through the predictions implied by them.[3]

In order to understand the abstract calculus which is the foundation of deductive logic, it is necessary to describe syllogistic reasoning.[4]

THE SYLLOGISM

A syllogism consists of two statements from which a conclusion is drawn; a syllogism therefore highlights the logical structure of an argument in which the relationship between the premise(s) and the conclusion is emphasized. Consider the following:

1.   All firms seek to maximize their profits;
2.   Retailers are firms;
3.   Therefore retailers seek to maximize their profits.

This may be stated in general terms as:

1.   All objects A have the property B;
2.   Object C belongs to the class A;
3.   Therefore object C has the property B.

The statements 1 and 2 are called the *premises* of the syllogism, statement 1 is the *major premise* and statement 2 is the *minor premise.* Statement 3 is the *conclusion,* which follows logically (is deduced) given the truth[5] of the premises. Such a syllogism, because its premises are assertions, is called a *categorical syllogism.* In contrast, a syllogism whose major premise takes the form of 'If . . then . . ' is called a *hypothetical syllogism:*

1.   If A is true then B is true;
2. A is true;
3.   Therefore B is true.

The major premise in such a syllogism is a conditional statement, and the 'If . . component is called the *antecedent* while the 'then . . ' component is known as the *consequent*. It is to be noted that the antecedent may contain many clauses, and we may write the hypothetical syllogism in very general form as:

1. If A_1 and $A_2, A_3, , ,$ and A_n are true then B is true;
2. A_1 and $A_2, A_3, , ,$ and A_n are true;
3. Therefore B is true.

This form of the syllogism plays a very important role in science, and therefore in economics, and in such a context the antecedent clauses are known as the *assumptions* (or *tentative hypotheses*), while the consequent is known as the *prediction*. In the context of the previous discussion, the major premise is the *universal law*, and the minor premise is the statement of *relevant initial conditions*.

A statement is said to be *logically true* if it is accepted as true purely for the purpose of argument; this contrasts with *material truth* (or *factual truth*) which is the quality of being true of the real world. It is to be noted, then, that given the logical truth of the major and minor premises, the conclusion is logically true; indeed, the logical truth of the conclusion is purely a consequence of the nature of the reasoning which leads to it – the logical truth of the conclusion is independent of the material truth of the premises. The premises may be materially true or materially false and the conclusion logically true; however, a logically true conclusion is necessarily materially true if its premises are materially true.

There are, inevitably, a number of fallacies which may be committed within the syllogism. Fallacies may take many forms, but two are particularly worth noting.[6] One of the most common fallacies in deductive reasoning is that of '*affirming the consequent*'. This is a formal, or logical, fallacy since it involves a breach of the formal rules of logic. Consider the following:

1. If A_1 and $A_2, A_3, , ,$ and A_n are true then B is true;
2. B is true;
3. Therefore A_1 and $A_2, A_3, , ,$ and A_n are true.

In this form, the minor premise is an affirmation of the consequent (not the antecedent), and while the conclusion *may* be true, it is not necessarily true. The rules of formal logic only allow a weak conclusion, which reads:

3. Therefore A_1 and $A_2, A_3, ,$ and A_n are not-necessarily-not-true.

This fallacy is the basis of the problems associated with the verification of theories, and will be discussed later.

The second fallacy noted is that of *post hoc ergo propter hoc* (literally translated as 'after this because of this'); this fallacy lies in the assumption that simply because one event, E_1, occurred after event E_2 then E_2 was necessarily the cause of E_1. In an evaluation of economic policy, for example, it is always tempting to conclude that a policy designed to achieve a specific objective was effective if it is observed that the objective has been met. Specifically, consider a policy of tight monetary control designed to reduce the rate of inflation; after the imposition of the policy, suppose that the rate of inflation is observed to have fallen and the policy maker then concludes 'the policy was effective'. This commits the fallacy of *post hoc ergo propter hoc*. Equally importantly, suppose that in this example the inflation rate is observed *not* to have fallen after the imposition of a tight money policy; is it then legitimate, logically, to conclude that the policy has been a failure? The answer is no, for this too would commit the *post hoc ergo propter hoc fallacy* – there is no way of knowing what would have happened in the absence of the policy (the inflation rate may have accelerated in the absence of the policy and then the judgement would have been that the policy had been effective!)

There are numerous other fallacies which may be committed, but the two instances given are the most important.

INDUCTION

Economists (of whom econometricians are a subgroup) use data in a variety of ways but particularly in the derivation of *general* results and of *general* predictions. Such use of data implicitly (or explicitly) utilizes the method of induction. Consider why it is believed that the sun will rise tomorrow. Such a belief is based on inductive reasoning which takes the following form: all observations of past mornings reveal that the sun has risen on such occasions; therefore the sun will continue to rise each morning. The characteristic of inductive reasoning is that a generalization is derived from consideration of a number of particular observations. To illustrate the close relationship between induction and deduction, it is possible to state the above inductive argument in the form of deductive syllogistic reasoning:

1. The sun has always risen on mornings in the past.

2. What has happened in the past will continue to happen in the future.

3. Therefore the sun will rise tomorrow.

This syllogism highlights the nature (and therefore the fallacy) of inductive reasoning. The observations which form the basis of induction (the major premise) are particular to a historic period and a specific location; however, the conclusion of inductive reasoning is a generalization which seeks to make some statement (prediction) beyond the range of the observations (data) on which it is based: induction seeks to predict what will happen in circumstances similar to its premises but at different points in time or at different places. To form the logical link between the major premise and the conclusion it is necessary to involve (either explicitly, as in the syllogism, or implicitly) a minor premise of the form stated above.

In inductive reasoning, the essential problem concerns the minor premise, for this requires an appeal to a 'Principle of Regularity' (that is, a principle which states, as a matter of faith, that what has been will continue to be). Clearly, if we were to be convinced of the material truth of such a principle there would be no objection to the material truth of inductively based predictions; unfortunately, any attempt to justify the material truth of the Principle of Regularity itself requires an appeal to an inductively based conclusion (which would require an appeal to the very principle whose truth is to be demonstrated). This circularity cannot be broken which is why the principle was described above as a matter of faith.

From the perspective of a scientist, it is important to ask, then, to what extent can inductive reasoning provide *proof*? Unfortunately, because of the nature of the minor premise, conclusive material proof cannot be derived from inductive reasoning, and the simple, familiar, example given at the beginning of this section makes this clear.

This logical problem of induction has concerned philosophers, and others, ever since Hume.[7] An inductively based conclusion cannot be said to be materially true since there is no way of establishing the material truth of the minor premise (that of regularity); the question to be answered is simply how, logically, one may infer anything regarding future experience when the evidence is nothing but historical experience.

It follows from the above that there is a fundamental asymmetry between induction and deduction. The problem of induction is that no universal statement may be logically derived, or established with certainty, from a finite number of singular statements; in contrast, a universal statement may be logically refuted with the aid of deductive reasoning from one single contrary event.[8] This naturally leads us to discuss the issues of verification and falsification.

FALSIFICATION AND VERIFICATION

Attempts to assert the necessary truth of a hypothesis because its predictions are in accordance with data drawn from 'the real world' are fallacious. In reasoning from the correspondence between a theory's predictions and material observations (the minor premise: 'B is true') to the conclusion ('therefore the theory is true') commits the logical fallacy of affirming the consequent. In contrast, there is a logical force to the process of falsification or refutation: if the theory's predictions are refuted by material observations (the minor premise: 'B is false') then it is logically valid to conclude that the antecedent of the major premise is therefore false. This process is known as 'denying the consequent'. The syllogism runs thus:

1. If A_1 and $A_2, A_3, , ,$ and A_n are true then B is true;
2. B is false;
3. Therefore at least one of the propositions $A_1, A_2, A_3, , ,$ and A_n is false (and therefore the theory encapsulated by these propositions is false).

Thus, while there is no logic of confirmation, there is a logic of falsification. As Blaug (1980) states: 'there is no logic of proof but there is a logic of disproof' (p. 14). From this asymmetry Popper formed his demarcation criterion between science and non-science, namely that science is that body of synthetic propositions regarding the real world which, at least in principle, are capable of refutation through the use of empirical observations. To quote Blaug:

> To verify the predictions of a theoretical explanation, to show that the observable phenomena are compatible with the explanation is all too easy: there are few theories, however absurd, that will not be found to be verified by some observations. A scientific theory is only really put to the test when a scientist specifies in advance the observable conditions that would falsify the theory (*op cit*, p. 24).

Science as a label, therefore, is independent of its subject matter, but is

characterized, rather, by its method of formulating and testing propositions; moreover, science is independent of the certainty which is attached
to its propositions. The line between science and non-science is, inevitably, a thin line and falsifiability is more a matter of degree than an absolute
criterion, a point which will be discussed below.

The context of science, then, is the generation and testing of hypotheses,
in which falsified hypotheses are replaced by hypotheses which, though
capable in principle of refutation, successfully withstand attempts to
falsify them. To Popper, and others, the source of hypotheses is not a matter
for inquiry, though he insists that induction is not a true source. This
position follows from the view that any set of observations itself is the
subject of choice: once a set of observations has been selected (from
amongst those which were possible) a particular theoretical perspective
has itself been adopted. All 'facts', all 'observations', are theory-laden;
thus Popper denies that induction constitutes 'unprejudiced generalization' since all observations are made in the language of some theory (if only
implicitly). As Chalmers (1980) remarked: 'Observation statements, then,
are always made in the language of some theory and will be as precise as
the theoretical or conceptual framework they utilize is precise . . . . Precise,
clearly formulated theories are a prerequisite for precise observations. In
this sense theories precede observations' (p. 27).[9] However, we all face
inductive arguments, and Popper's denial of induction is actually a denial
of induction as providing a *demonstrative logical argument*.[10] Only
deduction can provide demonstrative arguments; however, what induction
offers is a non-demonstrative argument which attempts to suggest that a
particular hypothesis is supported by the observations. Such presentations
of inductive evidence and their associated conclusions are labelled non-
demonstrative since the conclusion, while in some sense 'supported' by the
premises, is not a logical sequitur: even if the major and minor premises are
materially true, a non-demonstrative inductively based conclusion cannot
logically exclude the possibility that the conclusion is false. The syllogism
to illustrate this is as follows:

1. If A_1 and $A_2, A_3, , ,$ and A_n are true then B is true;
2. B is not falsified, nor has B ever been falsified;
3. Therefore $A_1, A_2, A_3, , ,$ and A_n are true.

It is clear that both the premises may be materially true, yet the conclusion
may be materially false. Nevertheless, such a syllogism, involving a non-
demonstrative conclusion, might convince some individuals.

Popper's denial of induction, and his assertion that 'induction is myth' is concerned with induction as a demonstrative argument, not with induction as a non-demonstrative attempt at confirmation. Indeed, Popper has much to say regarding non-demonstrative induction (sometimes called the 'logic of confirmation'[11]) but the important point to be made here is that the real contrast is not between deduction, on the one hand, and induction on the other, but between demonstrative and non-demonstrative arguments. Blaug (1980) is particularly critical of the ambiguous label induction. He prefers the use of the word 'adduction' to mean the 'non-logical operation of leaping from the chaos that is the real world to a hunch or tentative conjecture about the actual relationship that holds between the set of relevant variables' (pp. 16, 17). Thus, Blaug concludes: 'let us not say that science is based on induction: it is based on adduction followed by deduction' (p. 17). Further, following the deduction stage, science then proceeds to test the deductively based conclusions, replacing falsified theories by those which withstand the test.

However, the criteria which are used to falsify a theory are a matter of choice; moreover, if a theory's predictions do not conform to what is observed, the conclusion offered above is to reject the theory as encapsulated in the propositions $A_1, \ldots, A_n$. It may be that some of those propositions are 'true' while others are 'false', but the empirical evidence does not identify which particular propositions have been refuted. It is therefore possible for an investigator to declare that the case is 'not proven' against any one of the tentative hypotheses $\{A_i\}$; this illustrates Duhem's irrefutability thesis, namely that with regard to any one proposition, there are no crucial experiments. It is precisely because no such experiments exist that, in order to demarcate science from non-science, it is necessary to set methodological limits on the stratagems which are admissible in the attempt to avoid falsifying a theory.[12]

STATISTICAL INFERENCE

Statistical inference involves the examination of a sample of data in order to infer something about the population from which that sample was drawn. Many of the techniques of statistical inference are concerned with the testing of hypotheses, and in making such tests it is always the case that single hypotheses are never examined in isolation; rather, *a main hypothesis*, with its *associated auxiliary hypotheses*, is tested against an *alternative hypothesis* (which, too, has associated auxiliary hypotheses). The formal framework of testing typically labels the main hypothesis as the 'null hypothesis' and the presence and role of the necessary auxiliary hypothesis are not always fully recognized. Recognizing the composite nature of hypotheses being tested denies the practicality of naive falsificationism: if the result of testing is a 'rejection' of the maintained hypothesis, what has been maintained is not the main hypothesis, but rather the union of the main and auxiliary hypotheses.[13] Thus, only the composite hypothesis can be rejected, not the main hypothesis alone since the rejection could be because (at least one of) the auxiliary hypotheses are false, whatever the status of the main hypothesis.

The syllogism to describe this is as follows:

1. If the main hypothesis, H, and auxiliary hypotheses, $A_1, A_2, , ,$ and A_n are true then P (a logically derived prediction) is true;
2. P is not true;
3. Therefore H and $A_1, A_2, , ,$ and A_n are not true as a composite hypothesis.

The auxiliary hypotheses, *inter alia*, are required to justify the statistical testing procedure (such as the hypothesis that errors are distributed normally), and if a main hypothesis is tested and a 'rejection' result is generated then this does not allow anything else, logically, but a rejection of the composite hypothesis; moreover, the sophisticated falsificationist recognizes that, since it is possible for an investigator to be unaware of the full set of auxiliary hypotheses, even the most exhaustive examination of $A_1, .., A_n$ which still leads to a 'refutation' cannot be viewed as a conclusive refutation of the main hypothesis H: there could be other auxiliary hypotheses of which the investigator is ignorant.[14] Thus, repeated tests (perhaps with different data sets) which generate the same 'rejection' result do not allow a *certain* rejection of the main hypothesis; however, in order to avoid the use of immunizing stratagems, it is necessary to adopt methodological norms which do allow the investigator, in such circumstances, to declare that the main hypothesis is 'false'.

Additionally, it must be recognized that any statistical test which leads to a 'rejection' at a given level of significance is, of course, subject to a Type I error and thus, as Popper (1968) observed, probability statements are inherently non-falsifiable because they:

> *do not rule out anything observable*; . . . 'practical falsification' can only be
> obtained through a methodological decision to regard highly improbable events

as ruled out – as prohibited. . . Where does this high improbability begin? (p. 190 and 191, original emphasis).

In testing economic hypotheses, such as 'the variable Y is related to the variable X' it is the *negation* of this hypothesis which is examined as the main hypothesis of interest;[15] thus the null hypothesis is stated in precise language such as 'the population parameter in question is zero' and the alternative is stated merely as the negation of the null: 'the population parameter is not zero'. In testing the hypotheses, one against the other, the formal apparatus of statistical testing allows only two decisions to be made: either the null hypothesis is rejected or it is not rejected.[16] Either decision may be in error: thus a true null hypothesis may be rejected (this is known as a Type I error) or a false null may not be rejected (this is known as a Type II error). It is possible to attach probabilities to each kind of error. The typical approach to statistical testing is to set a low Type I error and then choose that test procedure which minimizes the Type II error; clearly the errors are dependent on the hypotheses under consideration.[17] The role of Type I and II errors is most important in the hypothetico-deductive method for two reasons.

First, the predictions of an economic theory are probabalistic in nature[18] and second, in assessing the material truth or otherwise of a prediction, the evidence is essentially probabilistic. This creates two distinct problems: first, probabilistic statements are, as noted above, inherently non-falsifiable since they 'do not rule out anything observable' and, second, as a consequence the attempt to falsify the minor premise of the deductive syllogism must utilize some specific methodological rule. Thus, in order to conclude that 'P is false' when the prediction P is itself probabalistic and when the evidence at hand is also probabalistic requires some 'norm' which effectively rules out unlikely events.

Take the following simple example: suppose that given a set of assumptions regarding economic behaviour, it is proposed that the measured observations on the economic variable Y are related linearly to the measured observations on the economic variable X by the parameter ß. This prediction is probabilistic in the sense that it is recognized that there are errors, approximations and omissions in this theory, the influence of which are encapsr 'ated in the error term, u, in the model:

$$Y_i = \alpha + \beta X_i + u_i$$

The error u_i is assumed to be a white noise term; this is itself a highly composite auxiliary hypothesis, and the relationship between the formulation of the regression equation (into a systematic and non-systematic component) and economic theorizing has been explained in Chapter 1.

A test of the main hypothesis of the theory is to examine the null hypothesis $H_o: \beta = 0$ against the general alternative that β is not zero.[19] Standard econometrics texts demonstrate that this may be tested by forming the statistic $t = b/se(b)$ where b is the ordinary least squares estimator of β and $se(b)$ is the square root of the estimated sampling variance of β. Under the truth of the model's assumptions regarding the non-systematic nature of the term u_i and also under the truth of H_o (that is, assuming that the auxiliary hypotheses are true, but that the null hypothesis is false), this statistic, t, is distributed as a t-distribution. Extremely large absolute values of t are most unlikely if H_o is true (that is, if the null hypothesis is true, given the truth of the auxiliary hypotheses), *although any value of the statistic is possible*. Thus, given the truth of the auxiliary hypotheses, no value of t is inconsistent with H_o; however, small values are more probable than are large values if H_o is true. Thus, in order to make 'falsification' an operational concept, values of t larger than a 'critical value' are deemed to be evidence of the falsity of H_o (and thus of the truth of the main economic hypothesis). Thus the critical value is chosen so that it is only exceeded (absolutely) with a low probability. Typically, this probability is chosen as 5 per cent. If the observed value of t, from the one sample of (Y, X) values, exceeds the critical value this argument runs as follows:

> this 'unlikely value of t' may be interpreted in one of two ways: either H_o is true but the sample is atypical or H_o is false. Given the low degree of belief (probability) attached to the first interpretation, here 5 per cent, the second interpretation is adopted.

Nevertheless, it must be recognized that the decision in these circumstances to reject the null hypothesis may be in error – this is the Type I error. Equally, any value of t is consistent with the alternative hypothesis and therefore a low value of t which leads to the decision not to reject the null is also liable to an error, namely a Type II error, for the alternative hypothesis may be true.

Thus, the only way to arrive at a position of 'practical falsification' is to view those events which are 'unlikely' given the truth of the null hypothesis as evidence on which to assert the falsity of the null hypothesis. Clearly, therefore, practical falsification is probabilistic falsification, for rejection of the null hypothesis under these conditions is liable to a Type I error. Nevertheless, the adoption of such a norm is the only way forward: this explains Popper's statement, quoted earlier, that 'practical falsification can be obtained only through a methodological decision to *regard* highly improbable events as ruled out – as prohibited'.

Importantly, however, the statistics used in testing hypotheses within a regression equation have their assumed probability distributions only when the auxiliary hypotheses regarding the non-systematic nature of the error term are true; thus it is necessary to have 'confirmed' the specification of the model before the main hypothesis of interest may be examined. This illustrates that attempts at falsification may only proceed once the specification of the regression model (with all its auxiliary hypotheses, whether they are stated explicitly or implicitly) has been 'verified'. This, therefore, implies that 'practical falsification' requires not only a methodological norm which sets the Type I error of a test, but also methodological norms which set the criterion for 'verification' of the testable form of the main hypothesis.

Thus the position of the 'naive falsificationist' is wholly improper: as has been explained above, confirmation can never be decisive, but equally, naive falsification can never be decisive. The sophisticated falsificationist recognizes this. Although neither verification nor falsification can ever be decisive, with regard to the testing of a main hypothesis the informational content of verification and falsification are quite different: a further verification of an often confirmed hypothesis has no information content.[20] In contrast, falsification of a main economic hypothesis does provide information – it indicates the presence of a problem and provides the challenge to address that problem.[21]

CONCLUSION

Since there is no demonstrative logic of either confirmation or falsification, no attempts to test theories can ever be conclusive, one way or the other: there is no certain empirical knowledge. Moreover, there is no way of ensuring that our current state of (fallible) knowledge is the best that is obtainable. This, then, sets the limits and the challenges to econometrics. The limits are enshrined in the knowledge that our beliefs constitute only tentative hypotheses; those tentative hypotheses are the currently maintained hypotheses because, given our methodological norms regarding falsification and confirmation of the framework of testing, they have successfully withstood attempts to refute them. The challenge to econometrics lies in the recognition that we cannot be at all sure those maintained hypotheses are the best which are available, and one of the most important roles which econometricians can fulfil is, therefore, in the search for and identification of better scientific theories of economic phenomena. However, what we cannot do is 'to pretend that there is on deposit somewhere a perfectly objective method, that is, an intersubjectively demonstrative method, that will positively compel agreement on what are or are not acceptable scientific theories' (Blaug, *op. cit.*, p. 28).

NOTES

1. The hypothetico-deductive model emerged, especially, in the work of Mach (1872 and 1883), Poincaré (1902, 1905 and 1909) and Duhem (1906); for further discussion of this method and its historical development, see Losee (1980) chaps 9 – 11 and Blaug (1980) Parts I and II.

2. The *explanans* (or premises) constitute a universal law and a statement of relevant initial conditions.

3. Universal laws themselves cannot be translated directly into statements about observable events.

4. For further discussion of the syllogism, see Stewart (1979), especially chapter 2.

5. 'Truth' here is used in the sense of logical truth. A distinction between logical and material truth is explained later.

6. For other fallacies see, for example, Stewart, *op. cit.*, pp. 20–9.

7. As Hume wrote 'If a body of like colour and consistency with that bread which we have formerly eaten be presented to us, we make no scruple of repeating the experiment and foresee with certainty like nourishment and support. Now this is a process of mind or thought of which I would willingly know the foundation' (1748, quoted from Hume, reprinted 1955, p. 47).

8. This is the position of the naive falsificationist; this view is criticized below and shown not to be a tenable position.

9. This view wholly undermines the position of the extreme inductivists, the *logical positivists*, who went so far as to say that theories only have meaning in so far as they can be verified by direct observation: since there is no such sharp distinction between theory and observation (or rather between theory and the statements which result from observations), this view is not tenable.

10. A demonstrative logical argument is a compelling logical argument by which materially true premises always imply a materially true conclusion.

11. Popper uses the term 'well corroborated' (1968, chapter 10) to describe a theory which has successfully resisted falsification repeated.

12. See Popper (1968, 1972 and 1976) on this point, and for a most accessible discussion of immunizing stratagems, see Blaug, *op. cit.*, pp. 17–20. The implications of this for econometrics will be discussed later, especially in Chapter 4.

13. This view has a long history, but still requires highlighting: Losee, *op. cit.*, reporting Duhem's views, remarks that 'He emphasised that . . failure to observe the predicted phenomenon falsifies only the conjunction of the hypotheses' (p. 166).

14. This is a statement of the Duhem irrefutability thesis which leads to the firm conclusion that conclusive disproof is a myth.
15. This is a requirement of the technical apparatus of statistical testing.
16. In this framework, therefore, rejection of the null hypothesis is equivalent to a non-rejection of the main economic hypothesis.
17. This follows the Neyman–Pearson theory of statistical testing. This approach also highlights the fact that any test of a particular null hypothesis is critically conditional on the alternative with which it is compared.
18. See Chapter 1 for amplification of this point.
19. This is not the only way to test the predictions of the theory.
20. Although it may be suggested that the hypothesis is either insufficiently well defined to allow non-verification or that there are but few states of the world which are inconsistent with that theory – if this is the case then the information content of the hypothesis itself is low.
21. The logical difference between falsification and verification leads to a difference in the information content of the two approaches; this view is often identified as Popperian (see, for example, Popper, 1968). However, this view is also central to the work of Kuhn and Lakatos: see, for example, Kuhn (1970) and Lakatos (1978).

3. Econometrics and Positive Economics

Empirical analysis in economics has a long history: its origins can be traced at least as far back as the sixteenth century when the 'political arithmeticians' led by Sir William Petty analysed problems such as taxation and international trade with quantitative information. However, econometrics, as we currently understand the term, is of much more recent origin, and is marked by the foundation of the Econometric Society in the 1930s.[1] In essence, this period was one in which there was optimism that economic theory could be given empirical content. Not only did it seem that economic theory could identify most of the important factors in modelling economic reality, but it also seemed that the methods of classical statistical inference could be used both to test economic hypotheses and quantify the theoretical parameters of economic models. For example, Haavelmo's (1944) celebrated work *The Probability Approach in Econometrics* argued that theoretical propositions could and should be formulated in the context of a well defined statistical model. However, the optimism at this time was restricted to 'the converted' who were relatively few in number. Despite the rapid expansion of econometric techniques their application to economic problems was relatively slow to pervade the profession as a whole. There were several reasons for this: it was partly due to the lack of adequate computing facilities but also it was due to scepticism concerning the value of such work amongst those outside the *cognoscenti*. For example, work on macroeconometric models at the Cowles Commission seemed to be bogged down with the problem of identification; and early applications of correlation analysis to economic time series had raised the problem of spurious correlation (see Yule, 1926). It was relatively easy for the sceptics to point to these problems and dismiss much of the work.[2]

It was not until the 1950s and 1960s that econometric techniques received widespread interest and acclaim throughout the economics profession. It was still the case that relatively few economists had been schooled in econometric techniques, but there was now a widespread optimism in the value of econometric investigations.[3,4] During the 1960s economists sought to influence government policy not only through economic theorizing but also through the supply of quantitative information: it was a decade which saw the blossoming of the applied econometrician as an expert consultant to government on a huge variety of economic and social issues. As is well known, the period was followed by something of a credibility gap in the 1970s: even the profession regarded itself to be in crisis.[5] By the 1980s, a renewed optimism about the role of econometricians is discernible.[6]

One focus of this chapter is the 1960s' optimism in econometric investigation. Two major influences were undoubtedly Milton Friedman's 1953 essay 'The Methodology of Positive Economics' and Richard Lipsey's 1963 text *An Introduction to Positive Economics*. Taken together these two economists informed (and converted) most students of economics to a so-called scientific view of their subject, firmly establishing the label 'positive economics' on both sides of the Atlantic. Positivism is the 'doctrine that positive facts and phenomena, not speculation upon ultimate causes, are relevant in scientific investigation' (Marr and Raj, 1983, p. 390).

FRIEDMAN' S POSITIVE ECONOMICS

Friedman's essay and Lipsey's book popularized the distinction between normative and positive statements and yet are prescriptive: readers are told what economists should do. Friedman conveys his optimism about the value of this approach in the following way:

> There is not . . . a one-to-one relation between policy conclusions and the conclusions of positive economics; if there were, there would be no separate normative science. Two individuals may agree on the consequences of a particular piece of legislation. One may regard them as desirable on balance and so favor the legislation; the other, as undesirable and so oppose the legislation. . . . *I venture the judgement . . . [that] differences about economic policy . . . derive predominantly from different predictions about the economic consequences of taking action – differences that in principle can be eliminated by the progress of positive economics* . . . Progress in positive economics will require not only the testing and elaboration of existing hypotheses but also the construction of new hypotheses (*op. cit.*, pp. 5 and 42, emphasis added)

At the methodological level, Friedman espoused the view that 'factual evidence can never "prove" a hypothesis; it can only fail to disprove it' (*op. cit.*, p. 9).[7] Furthermore, using 'work' to refer to a model's 'success' with respect to statistical criteria, he suggested the maxim that: knowledge of how or why a model works is unimportant if, in practice, it does work. The approach runs close to 'naive operationalism' and, in this context, Friedman often emphasized predictive power. Important to the developing popularity of this approach was Friedman's own demonstration of how to combine theory with quantification in his (1957) book, *A Theory of the Consumption Function*.[8]

LIPSEY'S POSITIVE ECONOMICS

On the other side of the Atlantic the first edition of Lipsey's book (1963) can properly be seen as a product of the methodological seminar group at the London School of Economics, M^2T (Methodology, Measurement and Testing). Founded in 1957, the group sought to present economic knowledge in falsifiable form and sought to argue that theory alone cannot be a sufficient basis for policy conclusions.[9] This was, arguably, in opposition to the antiquantitative stance of Robbins, then senior economics Professor at LSE.[10] Interestingly, testing was not part of the original concept, the main emphasis being on economics becoming a quantified subject: it was only after learning of Popper's ideas that testing assumed prominence.[11]

Lipsey's text stresses the desirability of quantification; the production of testable implications; and the testing of economic theory. It is almost evangelical in style. The book is prefaced by a lengthy quotation from Beveridge in which economists are criticized for not taking 'the point that the truth or falsehood of ... [a] ... theory cannot be established except by an appeal to the facts'; and in which Beveridge goes on to state that 'none of them tests it by facts'.[12] Lipsey's concern was a general methodological issue of how to judge the 'correctness' of economic theories and he sought to teach a new generation of economics students that they should look for answers in the empirical rather than the *a priori* direction. For example, he writes 'the theory of demand and price can have few applications to the real world without some empirical observations of quantitative magnitudes [sic]' (Lipsey, 1963, p. 161).

Lipsey's first edition proposes the label 'positive economic science' as a description of the method proposed. The definition of a positive statement is one which is based on empirical fact; this is to be contrasted with a normative statement which involves personal judgements. Therefore positive economics 'deals with statements that could conceivably be shown to be wrong (i.e. falsified) *by actual observations of the world* ... [it must be] ... at least possible to imagine factual evidence which could show them to be wrong' (Lipsey, 1963, p.5).[13] Several Parts of the book end with a chapter criticizing received theory, presenting the problems of measurement and the difficulties for specifying the empirically testable implications of theories. In these chapters Lipsey was often led to conclude that the theory being considered either did not yield a large number of testable predictions; or that it yielded few implications about questions of interest; or that testing it seemed to be extremely difficult.[14]

EXAMPLES OF THE 1960s' OPTIMISM

Nevertheless, by the mid 1960s, the lessons for the next generation of students were set: economics should be regarded as a quantified science and economic knowledge should be expressed in a form making it amenable to testing. This emphasis was particularly appealing for a profession already fascinated by Samuelson's (1947) *Foundations* which stressed the role of 'meaningful hypotheses' by which is meant propositions capable of refutation by reference to empirical facts.[15] Moreover, both Friedman and Lipsey had *shown* how to combine theory with quantification. Indeed, even in the mid-1980s it is claimed that 'a watered-down version of Friedman's essay ... is part of the intellectual equipment of most American economists, and its arguments come readily to their lips' (McCloskey, 1985a, p. 9).

However, the differences between the views propounded on each side of the Atlantic should not be ignored: for example, Friedman was criticized by members of the M^2T group for saying nothing about the criteria for a good test while stressing testing[16] almost to the exclusion of any other sort of examination. Furthermore, he was charged with complacency in that he 'far too readily accepts hypotheses as tested' (Archibald, 1959, p. 63). This was a reference to Friedman's observed acceptance of a great deal of economic theory without actually offering any evidence of their having been tested (Klappholz and Agassi, 1959, pp. 65–9). By the early 1960s, the M^2T view of Friedman's 1953 essay was that it implied an unacceptable degree of naive instrumentalism (see for example the debate in the *Review of Economic Studies*: Archibald, 1961; Stigler, 1963; Friedman, 1963; and Archibald, 1963).

Good examples of the 1960s' optimism in applied econometric work can be found in the early published work of members of the M^2T group,[17] for example Lipsey's well-known reconsideration of Phillips's work on the relation between the unemployment rate, the rate of change of unemployment and the rate of change of money wage rates (Lipsey, 1960).

Amongst Lipsey's objectives was an attempt to determine the proportion of the variance in money wage rates that is associated with the two unemployment variables.[18] It is of course well known that theoretical justification for the Phillips curve was undertaken only after the empirical phenomenon was published and this was Lipsey's other objective in the 1960 paper. It was in fact consistent with Lipsey's stated ideal order of proceeding: first, the researcher outlines the phenomena which require explanation; second, a model is developed to rationalize the available data; and then further implications or out of sample predictions are tested (see Lipsey, 1960; and Lipsey and Brechling, 1963).[19] At this time Sargan was something of a lone voice at the LSE in keeping the main focus of econometrics on critical testing of hypotheses (Sargan, 1964).

THE GREAT RATIOS OF ECONOMICS

As already noted, much of the optimism at this time related to the ability to uncover empirical regularities, good examples being the Phillips curve and the consumption function. Yet one strand of this literature sought evidence on 'fundamental ratios' in economics: this was the objective of the Klein and Kosobud (1961) paper 'Great Ratios in Economics'. The paper opens with the words 'Economists frequently base their reasoning on key ratios between variables. If these ratios are in the nature of fundamental parameters, simplifications of theory may result'. The paper studies five 'celebrated ratios of economics':

- the savings–income ratio
- the capital–output ratio
- labour's share of income
- income velocity of circulation
- the capital–labour ratio

Klein and Kosobud put these ratios to empirical test stressing that 'standards must be high, and stability or plainly systematic variation in ratios must be found in order to enhance their usefulness [for the construction of theories]' (*op. cit.*, p.173). Underlying their study is the optimism that empirical investigation could resolve the question of whether these ratios were fundamental parameters. The conclusions are strong:

- ' . . . the savings ratio is not a constant, but is on a *declining* trend' (p.178).
- 'Our estimate [for the capital–output ratio] . . . shows a significant downward trend' (pp. 179–80).
- 'A formal calculation of the trend in this ratio yields . . . that there is no trend in [the ratio defining labour's share of income]' (pp. 182–3).
- '[T]here is a noticeable trend in [the velocity of circulation]' (p. 185).
- Our series show a steady upward growth in [the capital–labour ratio]' (p.187).

Significantly, some of these conclusions ran counter to the empirical findings available at that time. For example, the declining savings ratio was to be contrasted with the findings of studies by Kuznets (1942) and Goldsmith (1955, 1956) which presented evidence of constancy in the ratio. While it is interesting simply to note this, the example is particularly apposite for an appreciation of the way in which some belief in fundamental ratios (or more generally relationships) continued to pervade the profession. When, in the 1970s, it seemed that the received relationship between savings and income had broken down, a great deal of research effort was directed to the search for the definitive statement on the nature of the relationship.[20] Similarly, the episode of 'Missing Money' prompted research effort on the demand for money function, much of which was based on the premise that a stable relationship was there to be found.[21] The seeming unwillingness of some members of the profession to accept that some of the 'Great Relationships' may not hold has of itself been a strong impetus to empirical research, and indeed economists have learned much from such analyses.[22] No economist would today run a regression of a simple Keynesian consumption function, any more than they would argue that Keynes's absolute income hypothesis has nothing to say. Economists have learned to take notice of applied econometric studies and one might argue that they would be misled it they were ever to ignore them.

DIFFICULTIES WITH THE 'POSITIVE APPROACH' TO ECONOMICS

Notwithstanding the above, the 'positive approach' (whether propounded by Friedman or Lipsey) was found to be wanting for economic practice.

Three main difficulties were identified:

1. Many aspects of economic theory do not imply either strong quantitative or qualitative predictions.
2. Economics is made up of interlinked propositions: thus the main hypothesis is insulated from testing by the range of ancillary hypotheses necessitated in making it testable.
3. 'Refutation' is difficult because hypotheses are probabilistic and errors (of rejecting a true hypothesis and of not rejecting a false hypothesis) are always possible. Formally, refutation requires the rejection of a theory if one is confronted with contrary evidence; however it is difficult to know what proportion of such incidences are required before the theory is rejected.

These factors[23] contributed to the view that econometrics could not result in the rejection of many (possibly any) hypotheses and therefore the emphasis should turn to estimation of the parameter values of economic theory and comparability through predictive performance.[24] But before discussing this it is helpful to dwell in more detail on the nature of the difficulties identified above: the first important set of difficulties relates both to obtaining testable predictions from economic theory and to the difficulty that some predictions are hard to observe (for example 'price equals marginal revenue in competitive equilibrium conditions'). Furthermore there is the pervasive difficulty of testing joint hypotheses: given the number of subsidiary assumptions made in an economic model, it is virtually impossible to locate the source of what has gone wrong in the event of a refutation. In Archibald (1960, p. 213) it is admitted that the attempt to state refutable propositions seemed to lead into a maze of 'alibis'.

The second set of difficulties relates to the difficulty of translating falsifiability into practice: Lipsey acknowledged this formally in the notes introducing the second edition of his text: 'I have abandoned the ... notion ... of refutation and have gone over to a statistical view of testing that... all we can hope to do is to discover ... the balance of probabilities between competing hypotheses' (Lipsey, 1966, p. xx). Lipsey had become sensitive to the problem of errors of observation (both omitted factors and errors of observation, but he stressed the latter) stressing that errors 'may always be present' (Lipsey, *op. cit.*, pp. xx and 51); moreover, he argued that because all empirical hypotheses are really probabilistic, the hypotheses necessarily admit of exceptions and therefore one cannot absolutely prohibit anything. Lipsey concluded that stochastic propositions are not strictly refutable (see p. 51).

Archibald, acknowledging that 'there are many examples in economics of serious and important hypotheses that are irrefutable'[25] (Archibald, 1966, p. 281) and 'much activity in economics is devoted to empirical work with hypotheses that do not satisfy Popper's falsifiability criterion' (*ibid*, p. 279) sought a 'solution'. He wrote:

> My own judgement is that many of the irrefutable hypotheses in economics are important, that they are incurably irrefutable for good and fundamental reasons [noted above], and that the activity of comparing them with observation is useful (too practically useful to be acceptably called metaphysics) (p. 279).

He advocated scientific comparison: the probable truth or falsity of a statement should be compared with that of another statement by appeal to observation, that is reference to facts. Thus empirical investigation of a theory required only that it be potentially comparable with pre-existing rivals, with constructed rivals or with the null hypothesis and in every case by appeal to facts. Archibald pointed out that R^2 is a comparative measure: 'It tells us how much better our fitted relationship predicts the independent variable than does its own mean' (Archibald, *op. cit.*, p. 292). Perhaps the most well known example of this style of scientific comparison is the comparison of Keynesian theory with monetarist theory carried out in Friedman and Meiselman (1963). Yet, as is well known, this study settled nothing, provoked much controversy and led to a debate on the comparability of reduced form models.[26]

Given the fact that OLS technology had been around since the early 1800s, it is interesting to see quite why the economics profession so readily adopted regression techniques some century and a half later, in the 1960s. Perhaps the strongest motivation came from the desire to resolve theoretical controversy; not only had the Keynesian Revolution given the profession a new interest in a range of macro-behavioural equations, but it had also given rise to the Keynes *vs* Classics debate which did not seem capable of resolution at the theoretical level. The macroeconomic data were now freely available and computing facilities existed to allow the analysis of large bodies of data. However, the vision of resolving disputes was lost in the difficulties of carrying out the exercises and was soon to be replaced by an emphasis on verification and forecasting: provided the 'evidence is consistent with the hypothesis', the econometrician was content that the exercise was both satisfactory and complete; provided the forecasts were not 'widely out of line' with the actual outcomes econometricians were deemed to be doing a useful job.

IS THE EVIDENCE CONSISTENT WITH THE HYPOTHESIS?

Economists used the concept of statistical significance to establish the nature of economic relationships and, to some extent, were preoccupied with structural autonomy. Research undertaken throughout the 1960s led to strong statements like 'the evidence in favour of the existence of a stable relationship between the aggregate demand for real balances and a few variables is overwhelming' (Laidler, 1971, p. 91) and 'there is an overwhelming body of evidence in favor of the proposition that the demand for money is negatively related to the rate of interest' (Laidler, 1977, p. 130). Such statements exhibit the high degree of confidence placed in classical regression analysis at that time. It seems that economists believed that they could establish whether a variable was worth including in a regression by noting the number of standard errors the estimated coefficient lies distant from zero; they could establish whether a relationship was stable through time by reference to the newly established Chow test (1966): their faith in significance tests was paramount.[27] When faced with 'poorer performance' of these equations attention was turned to reformulate them to capture short-term dynamics (albeit in an *ad hoc* way): the confidence remained as partial adjustment mechanisms, adaptive and extrapolative expectations formation became standard components of both the empirical and the theoretical models. Confidence grew as these new models could be used to generate multipliers relating changes in an exogenous factor (x) on an endogenous variable (y). For example, the relationship might be specified:

$$y_t = h_0 f(x_t) + h_1 f(x_{t-1}) \ldots h_n f(x_{t-n})$$

where $f(x)$ is a simple function of the exogenous variable. Economic theory was presumed to provide the form of $f(x)$ and some guidance on distributed lag structure. Econometric estimation was used to find values for both the h_i and the parameters of $f(x)$. A classic example of this is the parsimonious version used in the demand for money literature where the equation labelled as standard is[28]

$$(M/P)_t = \alpha + \beta Y_t + \gamma r_t + \theta (M/P)_{t-1}$$

derived from combining the equation describing desired (or target) holdings of real balances:

$$(M/P)_t = \alpha + \beta Y_t + \gamma r_t$$

with an equation describing adjustment to that desired level

$$(M/P)_t = (M/P)_{t-1} + (1 - \theta)((M/P)_t - (M/P)_{t-1})$$

Here the estimated value of θ is used to distinguish between the long- and short-run multipliers and to infer the length of time it takes for the money market to reach equilibrium. Developments of these models tended to focus on the specification of the $f(x)$, leaving the description of the dynamic behaviour to the *ad hoc* distributed lag characterization. This form of equation remained popular into the 1970s despite the *'ad hocery'* and despite the fact that by the end of the 1960s econometric investigations had revealed a disconcerting lack of stability for fitted coefficients (e.g. 'Missing Money' and the Great Velocity Debate).

THE FORECASTING PERFORMANCE

The other main development in the use of econometrics in the 1960s was the creation of large-scale macroeconomic models. Econometricians were optimistic that they could build simultaneous equations models of an economy and, with the increased availability of macroeconomic data, use them both to test hypotheses and provide conditional forecasts (useful for policymakers and any other body willing to pay for them).[29] In some ways this was a direct development of the Cowles Commission approach to econometrics, and a development based on 'a basic insight . . . [due to] Haavelmo . . . that any economic system should [could?] be viewed as a probabilistic process governed by the joint distribution of all variables contained in that system' (Hamouda and Rowley, 1988, p. 106). The move was successful in that most economists (and policy makers) attributed the macroeconomic stability of the 1960s to the successful application of economists' work by governments; moreover, the issues of economic policymaking taught to undergraduates were couched in this framework. The model builders responded to the needs (demands?) of policy makers by carrying out simulation exercises that identified potential consequences of changing exogenous variables like policy instruments. The *ad hoc* description of dynamic adjustment referred to in the previous section also became a characteristic of these models.

Indeed, as the decade progressed there was an increasing reliance on *ad hoc* amendments to estimating equations to satisfy the empirical standards by which they were judged and to yield acceptable dynamic predictions:

> The situation was accurately portrayed by Naylor (1971). 'Econometric models which have been estimated properly and are based on sound economic theory may yield simulation results which are nonsensical. That is, the simulations may "explode", and inherently positive variables may turn negative, leading to results which are in complete conflict with reality.' Further, using the most sophisticated estimation procedures, simulations occur that 'in no sense resemble the behaviour of the system which they were designed to emulate' (Hamouda and Rowley, 1988, p. 111).

While the textbooks continued the rhetoric of the Cowles Commission framework, the builders of large models were divorcing themselves from it by making pragmatic adjustments to their so-called structural equations.[30]

WHAT WENT WRONG? THE SHIFT IN EMPHASIS

By the late 1960s, with the development phase of the large economy-wide econometric models over, the model builders turned to comparative simulations.[31] The forecasting performance of the relatively complex structural equation models was not particularly good, particularly for time horizons greater than six quarters and the emphasis on structural estimation was correspondingly weakened. Simpler forecasting mechanisms gained in standing: these were based on either 'reduced form' models (for example, the St Louis model (see Anderson and Carlson, 1970) or the time-series characteristics of economic variables (using techniques developed by Box and Jenkins, 1970). The St Louis model expressed the growth rate of nominal income as (separate) distributed lag functions of the growth rates of money and government expenditure. It was seductive: the model is easy to understand, has some intuitive appeal and its proponents promised a basis for assessing the relative significance of monetary and fiscal policies (to be inferred from the relative sizes of the estimated coefficients). The time-series analysts (using Box–Jenkins methods) promised a relatively cheap, straightforward mechanism for the generation of forecasts. Enthusiastic economists learned about autocorrelative structure (of economic data) and stationarity in time series. Of these two forms, it is probably the latter which has persisted: the time-series models often outperformed the large econometric models and have served as the foundation of the now popular 'atheoretical macroeconomics' associated with Christopher Sims (Sims, 1980a).

Alongside these changes in emphasis was the general awareness that econometrics was not able to resolve economic dispute.[32] Economists who had hoped for the 'ultimate econometric test' have been disappointed. Indeed,

> an econometric model will seldom be sensitive enough, or the data 'pure' enough, to test a theory satisfactorily. So in the majority of cases the econometrician takes the theory to be true, or at least possible, and uses his model to clarify and quantify that theory . . . [There is a need] to point out the limitations of econometrics. Our toolkit of technical methods often seems so impressive that we think we can solve all problems with it; but we must beware of overconfidence (Hebden, 1983, pp. 9 and 11).

One need look no further than the literature on the aggregate demand for money function to see how the 'answers' to unchanging questions have changed markedly over the two decades since the early 1960s' econometric work: Compare Laidler's quote in the third edition of his text *The Demand for Money* with the two given earlier:

> The fact is that a decade ago it was possible to be much more confident about the robustness of our knowledge of the demand-for-money function than it is now . . . Not the least important lesson that monetary economists have learned over the last decade . . . is that our knowledge [from studies of the demand for money] . . . though by no means non-existent, is fragile (Laidler, 1985, pp. 146 and 152).

There are many reasons for this but important is the point that the statistical tools that promised an end to economic disputes could never do so on their own – too much has been asked of them. For example Morrison and Henkel write 'significance tests have severe restrictions and difficult requirements for use in any research endeavour, and both the opportunities for and the actualities of misuse are great . . . the conditions for the use of the tests . . . are not and cannot be met in most behavioral research' (Morrison and Henkel, 1970, p. 310). One particular example is the fact that the goodness/

badness of a hypothesis cannot be decided on statistical grounds alone; and the criticism of authors who do this is neatly summed up in the accusation that they confuse statistical significance and substantive significance.

The prescriptive message from Morrison and Henkel is to remind readers that important contributions are often made without statistical tests and that they should place greater reliance on 'the application of imagination, common sense, informed judgment, and the appropriate remaining research methods to achieve the scope, form, process, and purpose of scientific inference' (p.311). In the particular context of economics it is of course the case that major developments are made without heavy reliance on significance tests: indeed McCloskey (1985a) argues that while economists (especially in the 1960s) delighted in the rhetoric of significance tests[33] they were not generally *persuaded* by the rhetoric. He points to the style in which we persuade students of the law of demand: we rely on introspection, analogy, utility theory, but not much on econometric results (see p.58). The point is that economists (quite properly) do not rely exclusively on econometric evidence to form their understanding of economic behaviour despite the fact that they may continue to present their subject within the 'positivist' tradition.

But there is another underlying theme on the perceived role of econometrics in economics, one which has led some observers of the economics literature to note the profession's relative emphasis on theoretical and not applied work. For example in his Presidential Address to the American Economic Association, Leontief stated that:

> Continued preoccupation with . . . hypothetical, rather than with observable reality has gradually led to a distortion of the informal valuation scale used in our academic community to assess and to rank the scientific performance of its members. Empirical analysis, according to this scale, gets a lower rating than formal mathematical reasoning (Leontief, 1971, p. 3).

A similar view was expressed by Phelps Brown in his Presidential Address to the Royal Economic Society:

> the more abstract, the more rigorous, the more general, so much the more distinguished . . . In economics at least those who devote themselves to the direct observation of attitudes and behaviour have commonly been regarded as playing in the 2nd. XI (Phelps Brown, 1972, p. 9).

One reason put forward for the apparent low regard for econometric work was the limited applicability of the techniques to the questions of interest.

For example Worswick (1972) reproduced the remark that Samuelson once made about economists that: '[they] are like highly trained athletes, who never run a race [Samuelson (1947)]', and argued that the remark could be fairly made about some econometricians who are 'engaged in . . . making a marvellous array of pretend-tools which would perform wonders if ever a set of facts should turn up in the right form' (Worswick, 1972, p. 79). In similar vein Phelps Brown noted that 'Those who have to bear the responsibility for policy . . . do not trust the systems fitted by econometricians to establish relations or coefficients on which that policy can be based' (Phelps Brown, 1972, p. 2).

These views still have some currency today and certainly there is some evidence that mainstream economics journals continue to devote more pages to the relatively abstract, theoretical material than to applied econometric work.[34] However, it would be wrong to infer that the economics profession as a whole has lost interest (or is it faith?) in applied econometric work: there is a strong confidence amongst econometricians that they have something to offer. In particular, there are some four strands of current econometric practice which display this confidence: one derives from the Lucas critique, which has stressed the problems of structural autonomy; the others are each devoted a chapter in this book and are associated with the names of Leamer, Sims and Hendry.

NOTES

1. In addition, in the 1930s and 1940s, both the Department of Applied Economics in Cambridge, UK and the Cowles Commission in the USA were founded.
2. In a Presidential address to the Econometric Society in 1957, Haavelmo summarized the dichotomous early perceptions of economists as follows: 'Some people hailed regression technique as a miracle tool for surprise discovery of economic laws. Others sensed the danger of a mechanical approach and created the bogy of "spurious correlation"' (Haavelmo, 1958, p. 353).
3. See for example the concluding remark in Wallis's 1969 survey of recent developments in applied econometrics: '. . . econometric methods have an essential role to play in quantitative economics in general and in economic policy-making in particular' (Wallis, 1969, p. 792). Moreover, see the *Editorial Note* which prefaced an expositional article by Jack Johnston published in the *Three Banks' Review*: 'This article is of a rather different nature from those usually published in this Review and is more difficult to read. However, in view of the increasing use of econometric studies by both government and business, and the growing interest in econometrics among economists generally, it was thought that readers might value this explanation of the subject by one of the country's leading experts' (see Johnston, 1967, p. 3).
4. Although it should be noted that some econometricians were already engaged in public 'soul searching': see for example Orcutt (1952) and the comments by Koopmans, Tinbergen and Georgescu-Roegen which follow this paper.

5.   See for example Brunner (1972), a volume based on two conferences held in 1967 and 1968 at the Ohio State University; the purpose was to examine the then current state of econometrics. Some of the key papers of the conference were very critical claiming that 'the early promise of econometrics had been frustrated. To use the words of one of the participants of the conference, econometrics has simply replaced "sloppy sentences by sloppy equations"' (Kmenta, 1972, in Brunner, 1972). Needless to say, not all participants shared this view of econometric practices; what is significant is the fact that such dissention existed amongst econometric practitioners.

6.   Consider, for example, the view expressed by Hendry in his inaugural lecture: 'Econometricians . . . are a positive help in trying to dispel the poor public image of economics (quantitative or otherwise) as a subject in which empty boxes are opened by assuming the existence of can-openers to reveal contents which any 10 economists will interpret in 11 ways' (Hendry, 1980, p. 403); and again, the view expressed by de Marchi and Gilbert in their Introduction to the Special Issue of *Oxford Economic Papers* with the title *History and Methodology of Econometrics:* 'Econometrics is now a fully fledged and distinct discipline, lying between mathematical statistics and economics, drawing on the one and *indispensable* to the other' (1989, p. 11, emphasis added).

7.   It should be acknowledged that Friedman's essay was un-Popperian – at odds with his apparent acceptance of falsification. Friedman makes repeated references to confidence in and evidence for a hypothesis; he refers to testing as if its function is to verify. (See, for example, Friedman, 1953, pp. 9, 12, 23 and 28).

8.   This book was well received in some respects; for example 'Friedman's book can be termed one of the greatest advances of economics in the latest years' (Streissler, 1960, p. 164) and Johnston described it as 'a most valuable contribution' (Johnston, 1958, p. 435). However, reviewers also revealed a strong impression that they felt that Friedman had rather overstated his case (see, for example, Houthakker, 1958a; Johnston, 1958; and Streissler, 1960). Nevertheless, it would be difficult to argue that the book had failed to stimulate interest in questions about using empirical evidence to test hypotheses (see, for example, the debate in Eisner, 1958; Friedman, 1958; and Houthakker, 1958b).

9.   In his introductory remarks on 'The Use of This Book' Lipsey makes clear his indebtedness to members of the M^2T group when he writes 'In so far as the ideas and viewpoints expressed here are novel, they are the common property of all my colleagues who are members of the L.S.E. *Staff Seminar on Methodology, Measurement and Testing in Economics*' (p. xvi).

10. See, for example, the view expressed by de Marchi: '[The M^2T group] sought to recast economic knowledge in falsifiable form and proclaim this independence from the dogma . . . that quantification is not only diffcult [sic] but unnecessary . . . the goal was actually very specific: to replace Robbins's *Nature and Significance of Economic Science* as the dominant source of methodological ideas for British economists' (de Marchi, 1988, p. 141). However, this view should not be accepted uncritically; for example, in the discussion of de Marchi's paper, Hutchison stated 'I was rather surprised by the extent to which Neil de Marchi made the Lipsey–Archibald movement an anti-Robbins movement. In so far as it's positive economics, one of the good points of Robbins's book was how he insisted on the normative–positive distinction. For me this Lipsey–Archibald thing was that they were *too* Robbinsonian. In that they were proclaiming positive economics, they were being Robbinsonian' (p. 32 in *Discussion* in de Marchi, 1988). De Marchi replied: 'but they were concerned about what they took to be Robbins's antiempiricism' (p. 33 in *Discussion* in de Marchi, *op. cit.*). On the issue of Robbins being 'anti-quantitative' see O'Brien (1988): 'there seems absolutely no doubt that [Robbins]. . . was, and remained, extremely sceptical about the quantitative aspects of economics and indeed of social sciences in general. . . . yet there

is some qualification to this picture. Robbins certainly does not seem to rule out observation on all occasions; indeed he argued, in one of his famous articles, that it was necessary to resolve differences produced by inconclusive *a priori* reasoning' (O'Brien, 1988, pp. 35–6).

11.   Again see de Marchi (1988). At this time, the LSE was a major centre in the philosophy of science and Karl Popper was a central figure there. His view was that all scientific knowledge is tentative and that the accumulation of (generally experimental) evidence allows the scientist to reject hypotheses that cannot account for this evidence. One of Popper's graduate students, Agassi, was introduced to the M^2T group by Klappholz which would seem to have been an important step in the group's acceptance of Popper's views on methodology.

12.   Extracts from Lord Beveridge's farewell address as Director of the London School of Economics, 24 June 1937. Published in *Politica*, 1937.

13.   This definition is rather wider than positive economics for it also incorporates the falsificationist views of Karl Popper.

14.   For example 'the [marginal productivity] theory . . . does not easily yield a large number of testable predictions' (p.326); and 'there can be little hope of obtaining propositions about oligopolistic behaviour which are of real use in positive economics' (p. 221).

15.   There are several examples: '[homogeneity of the consumer's demand for money] is a meaningful, refutable hypothesis which is capable of being tested under ideal observational conditions' (Samuelson, 1947, p. 121); 'By a *meaningful theorem* I mean simply a hypothesis about empirical data which could conceivably be refuted' (p. 4); 'the statement is meaningless because it could never be refuted' (p. 84); 'the theorems enunciated under the heading of welfare economics are not meaningful propositions or hypotheses in the technical sense. For they represent the deductive implications of assumptions which are not themselves meaningful refutable hypotheses about reality' (p. 220 and 221).

16.   'Testing' here refers to predictive power (Friedman's emphasis was placed on the capacity of the estimated relationship to predict the dependent variable): it does not refer to testing the null hypothesis $\beta = 0$, for example.

17.   De Marchi (1988) lists some 26 publications which he regards as M^2T- related work: some of these are applied econometric studies.

18.   The fascination with attempts to estimate an aggregate Phillips curve was symptomatic of a major change in research emphasis compared to the early work by Tinbergen and the Cowles Commission. It marked the extreme concern with model *estimation* as distinct from model *evaluation*.

19.   This set of procedures has a strong pedigree in the nineteenth-century literature of Mill: for example, 'instead of deducing our conclusions by reasoning, and verifying them by observation, we in some cases begin by obtaining them provisionally from specific experience, and afterwards connect them with the principles of human nature by *a priori* reasonings, which reasonings are thus a real verification' (Mill, *A System of Logic* quoted in Darnell, 1981 p. 148).

20.   In the UK the personal savings rate was observed to rise in the 1970s, whereas in the USA the rate declined in 1975–6. On both sides of the Atlantic there were attempts to explain the changes in the savings ratio (see for example Coghlan and Jackson, 1979; Deaton, 1977; and Cagan, 1983, referred to in Hadjimatheou, 1987).

21.   See, for example, Evans (1988) and the references therein.

22.   There is nothing surprising in this; it is precisely the way in which one might expect knowledge to develop.

23.   The first important set of difficulties relates to obtaining testable predictions from economic theory. For example, Archibald had found that the need to specify a number of subsidiary assumptions made it virtually impossible to get testable predictions

from marginal productivity theory and the theory of imperfect competition. On the second set of difficulties, see the view expressed in McCloskey (1985a) that 'The doubting and falsifying method, enshrined in the official version of econometric method, is largely impractical' (p.14). On the third point, it should be noted that this was not new to Archibald; Popper had in fact *answered* it! For example, 'since probability statements are not falsifiable, it must always be possible . . . to "explain", by probability estimates, *any regularity we please*' (Popper, 1968, p. 197).

24.   As early as 1966 Archibald had argued that rival theories should be compared in terms of their predictive success and gradually many economists and econometricians moved towards this more relativist position.

25.   Archibald's claim – that there are many important hypotheses in economics that are irrefutable – is essentially based on the set of difficulties already enumerated in the text, although he stresses the view that 'a normally distributed error term is a characteristic of social science, and so, therefore, is irrefutability. More generally, whenever we have a distribution that gives non-zero probabilities over the whole range [minus infinity to plus infinity] . . . we have irrefutability. The crucial point is that *this holds even in the absence of measurement error: strict refutability cannot be saved, in social science, by improved instrumentation, or more accurate knowledge of measurement error*' (Archibald, 1966, pp. 286 and 287).

26.   See for example Laidler (1971) who argues the case that 'comparing the reduced forms of these two models is not a very useful test of their relative empirical relevance' (p. 80). Archibald was not unaware of the potential for comparisons being inconclusive (1966, p. 295). Lipsey's way of saying the same thing is: 'The choice is not one between theory and observation but between better or worse theories to explain our observations' (1966, p. 14). Then the problem to be faced is that theoretically defined variables can differ substantially from the available observed data; moreover the observed data may themselves be incorrect. Indeed published data are far from being objective facts against which theories are to be appraised thus striking at the foundation of 'positivism'.

27.   Pagan (1984) describes most applied econometric work in the 1960s and early 1970s in the following way: 'Four steps almost completely describes [sic] it: a model is postulated, data gathered, a regression run, some t statistics or simulation performance provided and another "empirical regularity" was forged' (p. 103). He goes on to criticize the approach.

28   The estimating equation presented in the text has been variously described as 'successful' (Laidler, 1985, pp. 245–6), 'usual' (Gordon, 1984, p. 404) and 'conventional' (Goodfriend, 1985).

29.   In his entry in *The New Palgrave Dictionary*, Pesaran describes this development as follows: 'Over a short space of time macroeconometric models were built for almost every industrialized country, and even for some developing and centrally planned economies. Macroeconometric models became an important tool of *ex ante* forecasting and economic policy analysis, and started to grow both in size and sophistication. The relatively stable economic environment of the 1950s and 1960s was an important factor in the initial success enjoyed by macroeconometric models' (Pesaran, 1987b, p. 13).

30.   In addition it might be noted that Christ (1975) was careful to point out the role of the *human* forecaster who forecasts by means of an econometric model. He writes '[s]ometimes [the forecaster] may believe . . . that the model is going to make (or has made) an incorrect forecast; in some cases he [sic] then may adjust one or more of the model's constant terms or slopes in such a way that (in his judgement) is likely to improve the forecast' (p. 55).

31.   See for example the publication in the *International Economic Review* of the papers presented in a symposium *Econometric Model Performance: Comparative Simula-*

tion Studies of Models of the US Economy. The papers appeared over three consecutive issues of the journal from June 1974 to February 1975. Many of the papers were developed in a working seminar on the comparison of econometric models which had been meeting for more than two years before the first publication. The models considered were: Bureau of Economic Analysis; Brookings Model; MQEM Model (University of Michigan); Data Resources Inc. Model (DRI 71); Fair Model (Princeton University); Federal Reserve Bank of St Louis Model; MPS Model (University of Pennsylvania); Wharton Mark III Model (University of Pennsylvania); H-C Annual Model (Stanford University); Wharton Annual Model (University of Pennsylvania); Liu-Hwa Monthly Model (Cornell University).

32. This is a feature common to single equation work and the large-scale econometric models. In assessing eleven models of the US economy Christ (1975) wrote '[the models] disagree so strongly about the effects of important monetary and fiscal policies that they cannot be considered reliable guides to such policy effects' (p. 54).

33. Good examples of the enthusiastic adoption of significance tests can be found in the New Economic History – cliometrics – of the 1960s. Strong statements about refutation were made; for example in the Introduction to the Penguin Modern Economics Readings on *New Economic History*, Temin writes 'much of the work of the new economic history can be seen as a refutation of previous generalizations about growth, as is illustrated by the first four sections of this collection' (Temin, 1973, p. 9).

34. See for example Morgan (1988) and Leontief (1982): Leontief analysed articles published in the *American Economic Review* 1972–1981 and focused on the proportion devoted to theory as compared to empirical analysis; Morgan updated this exercise to 1986 and compared the data with data compiled from the *Economic Journal*, 1972–1986. In summary 'Economics [as appearing in the official journals of their associations] devotes half or less of its papers to empirical analysis' (Morgan, 1988, p. 162). It remains to be demonstrated whether more extensive other analyses would support this general conclusion!

PART II

4. Traditional Econometric Modelling

Traditional econometric modelling is a label used to describe a style of modelling which has been commonly followed by applied economists but which has lately come to be criticized by many writers, including a number of econometricians.[1] It is important to note that none of the critics of econometrics offer any telling objections to what might be called the technology of econometric theory; rather they direct their criticisms at 'the actual procedures followed by the workaday econometrician in turning out the "applied econometrics" papers that appear so frequently in our journals' (Mayer, 1980, p. 166). It is clearly important to describe the 'actual procedures' followed by applied econometric modellers in detail, but this is not a particularly easy task since there is a great variety of practice, and 'traditional econometrics' is not well defined within either the journal literature or the standard econometric texts.[2]

When econometric practices were first adopted by the economics profession little, if any, attention was paid to the methodological foundations which underpin econometrics.[3] Notwithstanding this there was a somewhat superficial appeal to Popperian falsificationism and a hope was held by some economists that it would be possible to place economics on an empirical footing similar to that of the natural hard sciences such as physics.[4] However, the then increasing use of mathematics in economics and econometrics and well-meaning references to the work of Popper were, and are, insufficient to guarantee that economics is a hard science: what was lacking was a genuine methodological discussion of the way in which economics generates and tests hypotheses.[5] In particular, the rationale for (and full implications of) phrasing economic hypotheses as probabilistic propositions was incompletely understood; it was thought (or, perhaps, hoped) that the adoption of the regression model from the experimental sciences would provide economics with a rigorous and reliable method of testing hypotheses and decisively rejecting false hypotheses. This has not proved to be the case: as Mayer has observed: 'On all too many questions we are buried in an inchoate mass of seemingly contradictory evidence' (*op. cit.,* p. 173). There are various reasons one can put forward for this state of affairs, two of which are worth identifying: first, the way in which the regression model has been used has led to a very distinctive treatment by economists of the 'error term'; and, second, too little attention has been paid to the way in which deductive theory and inferential (data) evidence are used in conjunction.

THE ROLE OF THE ERROR TERM

The specific regression strategy used by economists of the 1950s and 1960s led to the (now) familiar ordering of the typical econometric theory textbook:[6] the reader is first confronted with a 'properly specified' single equation model which has fixed regressors and a zero-mean, non-auto-correlated and homoscedastic error term. In such ideal conditions the ordinary least squares estimation method (i.e. technique) yields the 'best linear unbiased estimators' (BLUE); deviations from the assumptions made regarding the error term invalidate the property of 'BLUEness': if the error terms do not each have a zero mean then the unbiased property of the estimators is violated; if the error term exhibits either autocorrelation or heteroscedasticity then the efficiency of the estimators is reduced; and if the regressors are stochastic there may be implications for both the unbiasedness and the efficiency of the estimators. The standard approach then proceeded to examine those estimation methods (techniques) which improve upon ordinary least squares (OLS) in such conditions and, having introduced the 'ideal' regression model, such texts proceeded to deal with the 'problem' cases. The 'problem' was very narrowly defined: if the original assumptions were violated then the optimality of the estimators derived by OLS was denied. This traditional textbook treatment then indicated that, as a consequence, estimation techniques other than OLS were called for when the distributional assumptions of the probabilistic model were shown to be unwarranted. This approach was (and is),[7] therefore, driven by the assumed distributional properties of the error term but failed to suggest that any correspondence existed between those assumptions and the nature of the underlying economic theory.[8] Moreover, the 'problems' were 'solved' in terms of developing alternative estimation techniques.

Since econometric theory had demonstrated the optimality of the estimators derived by OLS, applied economists sought to estimate their models[9] by this method. If any one of the requisite assumptions was violated then alternative estimation techniques were introduced (such as variants of feasible generalized least squares[10] and instrumental variable estimation[11]). This approach failed to discuss why the original specification of the equation (including the original assumptions on the error term) might have been incorrect, but concentrated instead on developing estimation techniques to be used in preference to OLS. Any failure of the assumptions of white noise errors was treated as an *estimation* 'problem' to be solved;[12] consequently, in reporting their applied work, investigators typically failed to describe the *process* by which a 'final equation' had been selected, and were content to report only the final ('successful') equation. Given this, applied work which reported one final equation might easily have been the product of running dozens of equations, all but one of which never saw the light of day but were discarded on the road to the 'one equation' deemed worthy of reporting.[13]

DEFICIENCIES OF THE TRADITIONAL APPROACH

There are obvious deficiencies of this crude approach; the most important deficiency arises because applied econometric work is, in this stylized process, entirely driven by 'problems of estimation', and while there was some appeal to the methodology of falsificationism, the practice was actually an attempt at verification.[14] The equations (models) were *estimated* (or corroborated) rather than *tested*. By using econometrics as a device for estimation, rather than as a device for testing, the truth of the hypothesized model was maintained throughout the process; only those equations which 'failed to refute' the hypothesized model were deemed 'successful'[15] and the process of re-specification and re-estimation (as the response to the perceived 'problems') was both insufficiently well detailed and insufficiently well understood in a methodological sense. Moreover, the evidence which was interpreted as signifying that the original equation required re-estimation[16] was, typically, not interpreted as a refutation of the specification of that equation but rather as a need to estimate the equation by a means other than ordinary least squares. Such practices have led to some warranted criticism of applied econometric practices which follow this stylized 'traditional' route; the criticisms are usually described, pejoratively, as 'data-mining' or as a 'fishing expedition'.

'Data-mining' refers to the practice, described above, of running a large number of regression equations which differ according to their specification (whether in natural numbers or logarithms for example) and differ according to the independent variables used. That equation which 'best supports' the theory under consideration is the one equation deemed worthy of reporting. The motivation for such a search is one of verification, and the 'poor' regression equations are discarded; moreover, the direction of re-specification, given a 'poor' equation, is data-determined (though typically this part of the process is not reported by the investigator). In such circumstances, therefore, one must agree with Leamer (1978) that 'without judgment and purpose a specification search is merely a fishing expedition and the product of the search will have a value that is difficult or impossible to assess'(p. 2).[17]

However, it is quite possible to follow a route which is a variant of the 'traditional' road which has a sound methodological foundation. The particular modification proposed here is that, instead of running regressions until a 'verifying equation' is discovered, econometricians should seek to falsify hypotheses and, to facilitate this, should adopt a well defined search strategy in which each stage of the process has a known and publicly stated relationship to all previous stages. This, then, replaces data-mining with a style of data analysis which is characterized both by judgement and by purpose.

THE STAGES OF AN EMPIRICAL STUDY

Consider the following stages of an empirical investigation:[18]

1. A prediction, capable in principle of refutation, is generated from a main hypothesis and initial assumptions (auxiliary hypotheses) through deductive logic alone.
2. The prediction is stated as a linear regression model and is tested through ordinary least squares analysis.
3. The regression residuals indicate that either the 'true' error term has the desirable properties which validate the use of OLS as an inferential technique and therefore the main hypothesis may be tested; or the error term does not have those properties in which case the main hypothesis cannot be tested at this stage.
4. If OLS estimation is deemed to be legitimate, and the main hypothesis has been tested it may be rejected or not rejected. If OLS estimation is deemed not to be legitimate this particular form of the testable specification of the main hypothesis is rejected.

This staged procedure may be elaborated as below and in Figure 4.1.

1.   From a main hypothesis and a set of assumptions (tentative hypotheses), $\{A_i\}$, a consequent, or prediction, B, is derived solely through the use of formal logic. This may be stated formally as:

If H and $A_1, \ldots A_n$ are all true then B is true.

The consequent B typically takes the form of a prediction such as: 'the economic variable Y is expected to be[19] related to the economic variables listed in the set X; i.e. in expectation, Y is some function of the variables X'. This prediction is a direct reflection of the main hypothesis, given the auxiliary hypotheses, but is not in a form suitable for either testing or estimation; however, making the approximating assumption that in expectation Y is related linearly, through the vector β,[20] to X allows the hypothesis to be stated as 'in expectation $Y = X\beta$'. It is important to note that the hypothesis is stated as a probabilistic hypothesis, and in order to test the proposition 'on average $Y = X\beta$', the 'auxiliary hypotheses' $\{A_i\}$ must be made explicit, and additional assumptions are also required. These include, *inter alia:*

- Only those variables deemed as the most salient are included in X. Hence the (deliberately) omitted variables[21] are, in aggregate or individually, deemed not relevant on average;.
- The model is phrased within a *ceteris paribus* framework; that is, the effects of all other potentially salient characteristics of the environment are assumed to be negligible. Thus all other possible influences are assumed to have no net effect.[22]
- In modelling the response of Y to X as a fixed, linear, relationship any consequent errors or approximations have only a non-systematic influence.

2.   Data are collected and the consequent B (phrased as a linear regression model), is tested. At this stage it is also to be noted that the theoretical variables Y and X almost certainly do not have exact protocol (material) counterparts; furthermore, it is to be noted that their proxies may be measured with error. To test the main hypothesis, therefore, it is necessary to invoke additional auxiliary hypotheses concerning both the adequacy of the proxies and the nature of any measurement errors.[23] To proceed with testing, therefore, it is necessary to translate all the above potential errors, omissions and approximations into a white noise error term, as described in Chapter 1.

Figure 4.1   The stages of an empirical study

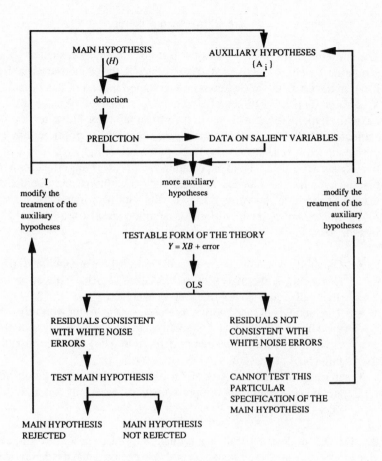

Routes I and II are not followed indefinitely; a final rejection of *H* results after the possible modifications to the auxiliary hypotheses all lead to either a rejection of the main hypothesis as a result of the regression analysis, or an inability to test that hypothesis directly within the regression equation.

3a. If the (joint) hypothesis that the error term in the regression model (written in terms of the measured proxies) is non-systematic is not rejected, the investigator may then, *and only then*, proceed to test the main hypothesis. If the main hypothesis is not rejected then the theory embodied in the statement 'on average Y is related linearly to X' is 'tentatively accepted' as a working composite hypothesis and the resulting estimates are taken as quantitative measures of their theoretical counterparts. If the main hypothesis is rejected at this stage then the theory may be rejected, though not decisively. (More will be said below of 'decisive rejection'.)

3b. If the (joint) hypothesis that the error term is non-systematic is rejected *then the main hypothesis cannot be tested within this particular equation* and the theory, as encapsulated in the statement 'in expectation $Y = X\beta$', is rejected,[24] though not decisively.

4a. If the conditions in 3a hold (i.e. the assumptions regarding the error term are not rejected), but the main hypothesis is rejected (because, for example, elements of the response vector, β, are not 'significantly' different from zero or have a significant sign in contradiction to that predicted by the theory), then *this particular specification of the theory is rejected.* It is important to note that what has been rejected is this particular algebraic specification of the theory, not the theory itself. Since the construction of the testable specification of the main hypothesis is the outcome of a number of decisions, notably the treatment of the auxiliary hypotheses, the investigator may recast the testable form of the theory (i.e. go back to stage 1 and modify the set of auxiliary hypotheses). This modification of the nature of the auxiliary hypotheses may take any of several forms:

- the peripheral behavioural assumptions may be modified (though not the fundamental behavioural assumptions since these are the object of the testing procedure);
- the set of regressors may be modified;
- the assumption of linearity may be modified;
- the assumption that the response of Y to its determinants is constant may be relaxed;
- different proxies for the theoretical variables (if they exist) may be used.[25]

This entails, therefore, a return to stage 1 and an iteration.

4b. If the conditions of 3b hold (because the error term does not exhibit the desirable non-systematic properties) then the main hypothesis cannot be tested and this certainly dictates that some modification of the treatment of the auxiliary hypotheses is required. This may take any of the forms indicated in 4a above and requires, as before, a return to stage 1 and an iteration. It is, of course, the case that the main hypothesis cannot be tested until the error term displays the characteristics of a non-systematic component; therefore the model specification stage[26] is of crucial importance to the testing of the main hypothesis.

The above illustrates the general point that any main hypothesis may be tested within a variety of specifications which differ according to the way in which the auxiliary hypotheses are treated; indeed, it must be recognized that the precise details of what constitutes the 'main hypothesis' is itself a choice. It is not a matter of choosing different theories until one is found that 'works' (in the sense of being not rejected)[27] but rather it is a matter of choosing the appropriate way of handling the auxiliary hypotheses.

A most important point should be made at this stage. It has been argued that a main hypothesis cannot be tested until the auxiliary hypotheses have been appropriately modelled; thus, in order to be able to proceed to test a main hypothesis of interest that hypothesis must first be translated into a regression equation which has residuals consistent with an underlying error process which is non-systematic. This, therefore, implies that before we may proceed to the stage of attempting to falsify the main hypothesis it is essential that we have confirmed the specification in which that test is to be carried out. Thus 'practical falsification' demands not only the adoption of methodological norms regarding the criterion used to deem probabilistic hypotheses as 'falsified'; but also demands a methodological norm regarding the 'confirmation' of the specification within which the main hypothesis is tested. This is closely related to the issue of 'pre-test bias' and will be further discussed below.

MODIFICATIONS TO THE ORIGINAL MODEL

In the sense that modifications to the original model may involve the addition of some variables to the set of 'salient' variables (i.e. expansion of the set X) this necessarily involves some modifications to the original 'main hypothesis'. Suppose that if, in specifying the original model, it was decided that some particular variables should be omitted because it was thought that their role was negligible; suppose further that the omission of some salient variables becomes apparent from econometric analysis;[28] the investigator may then, in re-examining the auxiliary hypotheses, decide that it was improper to have assumed that 'the net influence of the variables in the set Z is not systematic'; Z contains economic variables which, although potentially significant, were thought originally to play a non-significant role. This originally held tentative hypothesis is called into question by the data analysis and is therefore examined through the explicit inclusion of the variables in Z; the main hypothesis must now be extended to include a prediction of the response of the 'dependent' variable to the newly included 'independent' variables.[29]

The role of economic theory in this staged exercise is explicit: theory is at the heart of stage 1, and if the model is found wanting in any respect (either because the error term is found to be systematic or because that particular algebraic representation of the main hypothesis is rejected) then economic theory is crucial in the resulting re-specification of the regression equation by which the main hypothesis is to be tested. The act of re-specification is, however, crucial to the method of applied econometrics.

Since any main hypothesis may be maintained in the face of contradictory evidence[30] it is important to set the methodological limits on the stratagems which are admissible in the attempt to avoid falsifying a theory. To declare the case 'not proven' against a hypothesis because the testable specification examined is found wanting in some respects is an example of an immunizing stratagem;[31] however, to interpret such evidence as leading to a tentative rejection of the model as a whole, and therefore as prompting a re-specification of the testable form of the main hypothesis, avoids recourse to an immunization of that main hypothesis. Moreover, as described below, repeated attempts at re-specification, all of which result in a 'rejection' of the main hypothesis, provides a methodological rule which defines those circumstances sufficient for an hypothesis to be declared false.

The role of economic theory in the re-specification stages, and the role of inference as the prompt for re-specification, is explicit in the above description; both are essential components of the methodology of applied econometrics. Statistical considerations are used to identify the *need* for re-specification, but economic theory dictates the *direction* of re-specification; thus it is economic theory which is the driving force at each stage of re-specification. The specification of the original regression equation requires the assertion of a number of assumptions from which a main hypothesis is derived through deduction; the main hypothesis is then examined in a falsificationist mould within which the initial assumptions are treated as auxiliary hypotheses.[32] If either the auxiliary hypotheses or the main hypothesis are found wanting in any respect then the model is re-specified according to the dictates of economic theory; the re-specified model is re-examined and the process is repeated until the modeller's decision regarding the auxiliary/main hypothesis dichotomy is acceptable. Once this position has been reached the main hypothesis is tested;[33] if the main hypothesis is rejected at this stage the modeller may decide either to announce a rejection of the main hypothesis or may attempt to re-specify the model so as to make at least one of the auxiliary hypotheses explicit and expand the model accordingly. If attempts to model the non-systematic errors, omissions and approximations of an otherwise acceptable equation[34] lead to an extended equation which is acceptable in terms of the characteristics of its error term and the main hypothesis is still rejected, then the investigator may be left with no alternative but to announce a rejection of the main hypothesis. However, if the main hypothesis is testable within the first regression equation examined, and the test statistics indicate a rejection, this is insufficient evidence on which to announce a decisive rejection of that hypothesis. Because the framework within which any hypothesis is tested is itself at the discretion of the investigator it is inappropriate to announce a rejection at the first test of the main hypothesis and other specifications should also be examined before the decision to reject the main hypothesis is finally made.

PRE-TEST BIAS

There is, however, a technical problem to the above approach, and this concerns the phenomenon of 'pre-test bias'. Since all tests are of probabilistic hypotheses, no outcomes are ruled out; however, the model identifies some outcomes as less likely than others. All decisions (whether to reject or not reject hypotheses) are, therefore, subject to error; thus all re-specifications and consequent re-estimations and re-examinations of hypotheses are based on decisions which might be in error. This complicates statistical analysis and leads to a position whereby all iterative procedures of search are based on the tests carried out on previous equations. The correctness of the decisions made as a result of tests carried out on the finally chosen equation are, therefore, dependent on the correctness of all the earlier decisions made regarding all previous equations; if any early decisions are themselves in error then this will bias the later tests. This is the nature of 'pre-test bias' and is a technical problem which plagues all search procedures; the nature of the technical problem is one for statistical theory yet to solve and, at the moment, there appears to be no clear solution.[35]

The nature of pre-test bias is usually described in the context of the search procedure used (implicitly or explicitly) by applied workers who *modify* an equation by deleting those variables which appear, on the basis of a statistical test, to be 'insignificant'. However, consider an equation which is examined by ordinary least squares and for which all diagnostic tests of the error structure[36] lead the investigator to believe that the equation is well specified. Consequent on this the main hypothesis is tested and is not rejected using the usual criteria of statistical tests using a pre-specified Type I error, say 5 per cent. Is the claim that 'the main hypothesis is not rejected using a 5 per cent Type I error' justified? The answer, in fact, is no; this result may make econometricians feel most uncomfortable, but this is no more than a consequence of pre-testing. Since pre-testing the underlying distributional assumptions is a necessary part of the regression strategy, all subsequent tests inevitably take their validity from the assumed correctness of the decisions made at that pre-test stage. Thus any testing of the assumptions regarding the nature of the error structure actually invalidates the use of traditional statistical theory in the testing of the main hypothesis. What is invalidated is the assumed distribution of the test statistics (under their nulls) and, therefore, the critical values used to test those hypotheses.

As an example, consider an equation which is estimated by ordinary least squares and, among the diagnostic tests used, the investigator employs the Durbin–Watson test for first order autocorrelation; suppose the result of that test is not to reject the null of no autocorrelation. That decision itself is subject to a potential Type II error – it is possible that a false null has not been rejected. The immediate consequence of this observation is that all subsequent statistical tests of the fundamental parameters of the model are conditional on a Type II error not having been committed, and the actual distribution of the test statistics employed in the subsequent tests will only be as assumed when no error was made at the pre-test stage.[37] Indeed, the test procedure at the later stage will be valid with a probability given by the power (that is one minus the Type II error) of the pre-tests, and invalid with a probability of the Type II error; thus the actual distribution of the test statistic is conditioned both by the relevant null hypothesis and by the correctness of all pre-test decisions. Pre-test bias arises in equations which have not been the subject of modification, just as it arises in equations which have been; in principle there is no difference. A solution to this problem makes great demands on statistical theory – demands which cannot, currently, be met.

THE POWER OF DIAGNOSTIC TESTS

To address this problem, it is necessary (though not sufficient) to quantify the power of all diagnostic tests. Since the alternative hypotheses are typically composite this presents an enormous, and possibly intractable, problem. Even were the power to be known, it would then be necessary to combine the individual powers of the various diagnostic tests employed so as to quantify the power of the composite diagnostic tests. These requirements are not easily solved and statistical theory offers no formal route by which to incorporate pre-testing into the testing procedures of econometrics. This problem would appear to be so severe as to lead some to the conclusion that the textbook test procedures should be discarded. [38]

Pre-test bias can only be incorporated informally by investigators; thus applied workers should not interpret their equations (inevitably chosen through some search procedure) as if all decisions made on the basis of pre-tests were correct. Pre-test bias should, therefore, result in investigators interpreting applied econometric work with caution, as opposed to confidence. Leamer (1978) has criticized many applied workers for interpreting their work by effectively ignoring the presence of pre-test bias and proceeding according to 'The Axiom of Correct Specification'. This 'Axiom' describes the textbook characteristics of a regression equation, namely that in all respects it is well specified. Given this axiom, it might be suggested that the standard interpretation of the ordinary least squares could be adopted; however, as has been described above, the 'standard interpretations' are *only* available if the investigator is prepared to believe, as a matter of faith,[39] that the specification used is the correct specification and does not make any tests of the implied set of composite assumptions!

CONCLUSION

This chapter has sought to offer a description of econometric modelling procedures as carried out especially in the 1950s, 1960s and 1970s and to offer a variant of 'traditional econometric modelling' which seeks to address some of its more obvious shortcomings. From a methodological standpoint, 'traditional econometric modelling' is open to many criticisms for it was driven by statistical criteria and the purpose of applied econometrics became focused on the *estimation of models* rather than the *testing of economic hypotheses*. The spirit of those investigations was more in the vein of verification than falsification. This chapter has also shown how, with few changes, 'traditional modelling' may be placed on a sound methodological footing.

Notwithstanding this, the very difficult problem of pre-testing plagues precise statistical interpretation of any regression equation and the response to a recognition of pre-test bias can only be informal. Furthermore, the recognition actually denies the traditional formal statistical interpretations of test statistics. This drives applied econometrics towards a personalistic, judgemental, role in economics: it is still possible to speak of 'degrees of belief' regarding the truth or falsity of any particular hypothesis, but to speak of 'rejection at 5 per cent' is denied since pre-testing is an essential component of the machinery of statistical testing. The outcome is, therefore, that econometrics can offer evidence on which hypotheses may be rejected, but the criteria must themselves be based on methodological norms; the formal apparatus of statistics is extremely useful in this process, of course, but it does not provide unambiguous, well defined, rules of refutation.

That practical falsification can only be achieved through the adoption of methodological norms was originally recognized by Popper; his argument was based on the fact that probabilistic hypotheses rule out nothing observable. This chapter has shown that we also need to utilize methodological norms to accommodate pre-testing, and if later tests are to be based on distributions whose assumed 'truth' is decided on by reference to a pre-test, then we must adopt the methodological norm that no Type II errors have been committed at the pre-test stages. To the extent that this is difficult to accept, caution should be exercised in interpreting the results of applied econometrics.[40]

NOTES

1. The most notable criticisms from econometricians are those of Sims, Leamer and Hendry; their particular contributions are discussed in some detail in later chapters of this book.
2. Two of the most complete (personal) outlines of 'traditional econometric modelling' are provided by Hendry (1979 and 1985) and Gilbert (1986). Both authors provide an alternative label: Hendry uses the label 'specific to general' as synonymous with traditional modelling while Gilbert, acknowledging that he has erected a 'straw man' invents the '*Average Economic Regression* (AER)' view of econometrics (p. 284).

3. This contradicts the view expressed by Walters (1986, p. 119) in which he reports Klein's early (undated, though undoubtedly originating in the 1960s) complaint that there was 'a considerable imbalance between the vast energy devoted to statistical methodology and the little work that was being done in developing data and using the models empirically.' Walters goes on: 'As a managing editor of the *Review of Economic Studies* in the late 1960s and early 1970s, I was struck by the paucity of respectable articles in applied econometrics, compared with the ever-rising pile of mathematical theory and methodological contributions' (p. 119). Walters suffers, in common with many other commentators on the state of economics and econometrics, from a failure to distinguish method (in the sense of technique) from methodology. Certainly the 1960s and 1970s were characterized by a marked growth in the plethora of econometric techniques; however, there was a dearth of contributions to the issue of the *methodological* status of econometrics as a part of the methodology of economics.

4. See Mayer (1980) for a particularly stimulating discussion of the claims which economics has to be a hard science.

5. Indeed, references to Popperian falsificationism concerned more the role of econometrics than the methodology of econometrics.

6. See, for example, the popular undergraduate course texts by Johnston (1963, 1972 and 1984), Wonnacott and Wonnacott (1970 and 1979) and Koutsoyiannis (1973 and 1977). Koutsoyiannis actually distinguishes between two approaches: the 'orthodox' and the 'experimental'; in the former, the maintained hypothesis is maintained in face of any empirical results, and the investigator resorts to immunizing stratagems, whereas in the latter 'the econometrician experiments with various *theoretically plausible models*' (p. 23, our emphasis). Neither approach, therefore, is in the spirit of attempts to falsify economic hypotheses. Two additional texts are worth noting: Walters (1968) appears to make no reference to an equation other than a *properly specified equation* and does not refer to the assumptions required for regression analysis whereas Christ (1966) offers explicit discussion of the nature of econometrics within economics, and seeks to integrate economic theory and empirical modelling largely within a simultaneous equation system.

7. It is to be noted that this approach is that followed by some of the more recent texts: see, for example, the third edition of Johnston (1984).

8. This echoes the view of Hendry (1985): 'Conventional modelling assumes that the model and data process coincide at the outset; i.e. that the data were actually generated by the factors in the model *plus a random innovation impinging from nature*' (p. 75, our emphasis).

9. The estimation of models was largely within the context of a single equation; simultaneous systems did not enjoy such widespread popularity. Even when a simultaneous approach was thought appropriate, some investigators demonstrated that they lacked a full understanding of the procedures: see, for example, the study by Lipsey and Parkin (1970) who, in a two-equation model of prices and wages, declare that two - stage least squares cannot be used because to do so would require the assumption that those variables exogenous to the two equations in question were also exogenous to the macroeconomic system as a whole. (For a criticism and discussion of this issue, see, for example, Hebden, 1983, pp. 175–87.)

10. In the case when the errors exhibited either autocorrelation or heteroscedasticity, techniques such as the Cochrane–Orcutt method and weighted least squares were developed, respectively.

11. This technique was developed as a 'solution' to the 'problem' of dependence between the errors and the regressors.

12. Rather than as an indication of model mis-specification.

13. Only the 'successful' equations were reported. This is hardly surprising at one level –

referees and journal editors have a natural inclination to publish 'successful' work, but this inevitably masked the specification search process which led to the final equation. In the knowledge that journals reported 'successful' equations, authors may have felt a reluctance to describe the process which led to their conclusions. The end product was seen as more important than the process; indeed, it is not clear that the process was seen as important at all.

14. See, for example, Koutsoyiannis (1977): 'Econometrics aims primarily at the verification of economic hypotheses' (p. 8).

15. It is to be noted that 'success' is often measured by the goodness-of-fit and by the number of 'significant' coefficients in an equation; in this context significance means that on statistical grounds a coefficient is deemed to be different from zero. To the extent that the maintained hypothesis identifies those coefficients which are non-zero this constitutes a falsificationist approach; however, to the extent that the driving force of applied work was to discover and report those equations which failed to refute the maintained hypothesis, this search procedure is a crude attempt at verification .

16. Typically, the most important statistic used as an indicator that OLS was not appropriate was the Durbin–Watson statistic.

17. A most interesting paper by Lovell (1983) has examined the statistical properties of estimators derived from data-mining; his conclusions demonstrate that the reported Type I errors from such a strategy are improperly reported and always lead to exaggerated claims of significance. He also provides some simple rules of thumb by which to deflate such claims. The source of the exaggeration is 'pre-test bias', a phenomenon explained later in this chapter.

18. This discussion is in terms of a single equation, though the extension to a simultaneous equation system is not at all difficult.

19. The phrase 'is expected to be' is to be interpreted within the usual phrasing of *ceteris paribus* clauses.

20. Economic theory typically provides predictions of the sign of the individual elements of ß.

21. The investigator will be aware of some of the potentially salient variables which have been omitted, but may also be ignorant of many others. Nevertheless, whether the investigator is or is not aware of the complete list of omitted relevant variables the decision to omit is made positively, and in this sense the omitted variables are 'deliberately omitted'.

22. 'No net effect' is translated into the statistical requirement that all other potential effects have no systematic influence.

23. Specifically, the linear equation relating the observed values of the proxy variable for Y to the observed values of the proxies chosen for X is assumed to have an additive error term (encapsulating all errors, omissions and approximations) which is assumed to behave as if it were a white noise random variable and the regressors are independent of the errors; i.e. the errors are assumed to have a wholly non-systematic influence.

24. This, too, echoes Hendry (1985): '*any* misfit (between the estimated equation and the observations) should lead to rejection of the model' (p. 75, original emphasis).

25. These possible modifications are neither mutually exclusive nor exhaustive.

26. Model specification is a wide term which includes the specification of both the systematic and the non-systematic component of the dependent variable. In fact, the specification of the systematic component requires the specification of the functional form, the variables to be explicitly included, the proxies to be used and the constancy of the response vector; this necessarily constrains the nature of the errors omissions and approximations and therefore identifies, through subtraction, that part of the determination of Y which has not been modelled explicitly, Clearly, if the systematic component of Y is modelled as $X\beta$ then the non-systematic component, u, is simply given by $u = Y - X\beta$. This 'definition' of u is tautological, and any test of the main

hypothesis requires explicit assumptions of the non-systematic character of the error term u (through consideration of the treatment of the auxiliary hypotheses).

27. This is largely the substance of the current criticisms of traditional modelling as practised in the 1950s and early 1960s: as Blaug (1980) observes 'much of it [empirical research] is like playing tennis with the net down: instead of attempting to refute testable predictions, modern economists all too frequently are satisfied to demonstrate that the real world conforms to their predictions, thus replacing falsification, which is difficult, with verification, which is easy' (p. 256).

28. Omission of some variables may be indicated by, for example, the presence of autocorrelation in the residuals or by the apparent 'breakdown' of an equation through predictive failure or by a poor fit to the sample data or by the presence of heteroscedasticity in the residuals. This list is not intended to be exhaustive.

29. The original main hypothesis regarding the sign of responses between the 'dependent' and 'independent' variables remains unchanged.

30. This follows from the irrefutability thesis; all hypotheses which are tested are actually composite, not single hypotheses, and the investigator may choose to use a 'slack' methodological norm to indicate rejection.

31. See Chapter 2 for further discussion of immunizing stratagems.

32. The assumptions, treated as auxiliary hypotheses, are implicitly testable through their implications for a non-systematic error term.

33. It is of vital importance to note that the main hypothesis cannot be tested until the auxiliary hypotheses have been appropriately specified such that the errors, omissions and approximations associated with the equation have only a non-systematic influence.

34. An 'otherwise acceptable equation' here means one in which the error behaves as a non-systematic component but one in which the main hypothesis of interest is rejected.

35. For a particularly clear explanation of pre-test bias, see Kennedy (1985). With reference to the earlier discussion of data-mining, it is interesting to note Kennedy's view that: 'The most dramatic implication of the pre-test bias phenomenon occurs when econometricians use sequential or "step-wise" testing procedures' (p. 159).

36. For a description of various diagnostic tests see, for example, the brief statements in Pesaran and Pesaran (1987) pp. 136–9 and the references cited there.

37. This also means that the critical values used are only correct when no Type II error was made at the pre-test stage.

38. See, for example, Leamer (1978) pp. 4–5.

39. That is, not as a result of any pre-tests. This procedure would then be open to the charge that the investigator simply does not know whether or not the test statistics are valid, and is, therefore, not recommended.

40. As Theil (1971) observed: 'the most sensible procedure is to interpret confidence intervals and significance limits liberally when confidence intervals and test statistics are computed from the final regression of a regression strategy' (p. 605).

5. 'General to Specific' Modelling: Hendry's Contributions to Econometrics*

Over recent years it has become increasingly fashionable to study economic time-series data using the econometric methods of dynamic autoregressive distributed lag modelling, as proposed and popularized by Hendry and Mizon. In a series of papers (see especially Mizon, 1977; Hendry and Mizon, 1978; Hendry, 1979; and Hendry, 1980) these authors have criticized what are labelled the more 'traditional' methods of econometric practice[1] and have championed an alternative approach, labelled 'general to specific' modelling. This technique has been readily adopted by many of the influential model builders and a number of econometric relationships have been investigated through this modelling procedure (see, for example, Davidson et al., 1978; and Rose, 1985). The technique has also been used by Hendry and Ericsson (1983) to launch a major criticism of the work of Friedman and Schwartz (1982). Also, McAleer et al. (1985), in a highly critical review of Leamer's work[2] have advocated the principles of 'general to specific' modelling in very positive terms for, they argued, such principles, 'consistently applied . . . can go a long way towards the "de-conning" of econometrics' (p. 294). This view is examined in detail below.

The work by Spanos (1986) has much in common with, and is a development of, Hendry's work. In particular, Spanos utilizes the notion of the 'Data Generating Process' (DGP) and highlights the role of the observed data in specifying the statistical model. This approach, like that of Hendry, has roots which go back to Sargan's work on prices and wages (1964) in which a prominent role was assigned to the temporal nature of the data in specifying the finally chosen equation.

There may be an advantage, for some purposes, in distinguishing between 'the econometrics of Hendry' and 'Hendrification'; however, that possible distinction is not the focus of attention. This chapter seeks to demonstrate that the results of 'general to specific' modelling (i.e. what

* A longer version of this chapter is to be found in Darnell (1989).

might be called the results of 'Hendrification') require rather more careful interpretation than has typically been the case; more importantly, it seeks to demonstrate that dynamic specification and estimation (i. e. what might be called the 'econometrics of Hendry') do not provide a framework within which economic theories may be tested and, therefore, are capable of adding little to our understanding of economic phenomena.

'GENERAL TO SPECIFIC' MODELLING

Following the Hendry–Mizon approach, suppose that economic theory leads to the following 'long-run equilibrium relationship':

$$y_t = \alpha x_t \tag{1}$$

where y_t and x_t are economic variables, assumed throughout to be measured in logarithms.[3] Within this modelling approach, economic theory is viewed as generating statements of 'long-run equilibrium' behaviour but it is assumed that economic data (whatever their frequency and implicit averaging) are generated by a disequilibrium process. In order to capture 'short-run dynamic adjustment behaviour' equation (l) is augmented by lags and is rewritten in dynamic, autoregressive distributed lag (ADL) form:

$$y_t = \sum_{j=0}^{m} (\beta_j x_{t-j} + \delta_j y_{t-1-j}) \tag{2}$$

Using the lag operator L, (2) may be written in obvious notation as:

$$\delta(L) y_t = \beta(L) x_t \tag{3}$$

To estimate this equation, an error term is added and the maximum lag length, m, is chosen.[4] Equation (3) represents the 'most general model' and is an 'intended overparameterization'; by 'data based simplification'[5] it is reduced to a more parsimonious equation. Hendry and Richard (1983) offered six criteria which, they suggested, the simplified specification ought to satisfy. They proposed that the simplified equation should:[6]

• be *data-admissible*. This requires that it is logically possible for the data to have generated the specification chosen;[7]

- be *consistent* with theory. This criterion will be examined in detail below;
- have regressors which are at least *weakly exogenous.*[8] Were this not the case then the variables which violate weak exogeneity should be modelled jointly;
- exhibit *parameter constancy.* Clearly, if it is intended to use the equation successfully in forecasting or for policy simulation then this is a basic requirement;
- be *data-coherent.* Essentially this requires that the actual residuals are consistent with a white noise true error structure;
- *encompass* all rival models. This means that the equation must be capable of explaining the results of other specifications.

Such characteristics are not sufficient for an equation to represent an acceptable economic theory; indeed, they may not even be necessary.[9] For example, the search for an equation which exhibits parameter constancy may not be necessary. If the economic phenomenon under consideration has actually experienced a structural break, but the investigator seeks a relationship which is wholly stable, then it is not beyond the wit of an econometrician to model the phenomenon in autoregressive distributed lag form as if it were stable.[10] Moreover, if the investigator wishes to test the hypothesis of a structural break, then the Hendry–Richard proposals, which deny a break, effectively deny such an hypothesis *a priori.* The purpose here, however, is not to comment in detail on each of these criteria but rather to concentrate on the relationship between economic theory and the empirically based equation selection procedures of Hendry, Mizon and Richard (and the related procedures developed by Spanos).

Autoregressive distributed lag modelling proceeds by estimating the parameters of $\delta(L)$ and $\beta(L)$ statistically; their forms are then simplified using sequential tests, and the final form of equation chosen will, within this modelling strategy, be such as to meet all six criteria. Naturally, this approach to specification yields an equation involving lags of all the variables; however, economic theory has little to say about the parameters of lagged responses and so the implied long-run steady-state forms are derived in order to recover the link between this econometric exercise and economic theory.[11] The two steady states of interest are those which apply to the static case when the independent variable (x) is fixed over time, and the dynamic case when that variable grows at some constant rate.

Setting $x_t = x_0$ for all t and assuming stability, the long-run *static* equilibrium is given by:

$$y_t = \phi_0^{-1} \phi x_0 = \sigma x_0 \qquad (4)$$

where $\phi_0 = 1 - \sum_{j=0}^{m} \delta_j$; $\phi = \sum_{j=0}^{m} \beta_j$ and $\sigma = \phi_0^{-1} \phi$.

Thus we see that equation (3) has the long-run static properties of equation (1) with $\alpha = \sigma$. The long-run *dynamic* equilibrium is examined by setting $(1 - L) x_t = \pi$ and setting $(1 - L) y_t = \pi_0$ for all t; π_0 and π are proportionate rates of growth since the variables are in logarithms. Assuming dynamic stability:[12]

$$\pi_0 = \sigma \pi \qquad (5)$$

and $\quad y_t = \phi_0^{-1} [\phi x_t - \phi_0^{-1} (\phi_0 \theta + \phi \theta_0) \pi]$, i.e.

$$y_t = \sigma(x_t - \mu \pi) \qquad (6)$$

where $\theta_0 = \sum_{j=0}^{m} (j+1) \delta_j$; $\theta = \sum_{j=0}^{m} j \beta_j$ and $\mu = (\theta / \phi) + (\theta_0 / \phi_0)$.

This is described as the long-run dynamic equilibrium equation,[13] and to quote Currie (1981), it 'incorporates all the terms included in the static relationship (1), but includes in addition terms in the rate of change [of the independent variable]' (p. 706). The 'additional' dependence of y_t on π is viewed by Currie as a disadvantage of the approach, and he devotes much energy to examining ways of avoiding such dependence. In fact, the efforts are misdirected, for so long as attention is concentrated on 'long-run dynamic equilibrium' the dependence of the equilibrium path of y_t on π is assured. This remark follows directly from the linear dependence between x_t and π in 'long-run dynamic equilibrium'. Consequently, equation (6) is, perhaps, misleading as a description of the long-run dynamic equilibrium since it contains two arguments which are linearly dependent through the relationship which describes the long-run path of the independent variable:[14]

$$x_t = x_0 + \pi t \qquad (7)$$

Within this econometric method of equation specification, the link with economic theory is largely through the derived equilibrium relationships (the steady-state equations (4) and (6)) and it is their form which is used in the application of the second criterion, namely that the equation finally selected should *be consistent* with theory. It is most important to note that this approach does not involve an attempt at falsification, but rather uses verification as a criterion. This point will be explored in more detail below.

This modelling strategy, then, comprises several elements: first, statements of equilibrium economic theory are viewed as providing an inadequate starting point for empirical analysis since it is *assumed* that the economic data available reflect a disequilibrium process; second, it is *assumed* that that process may be adequately proxied by the use of lags of those variables already nominated for inclusion in the equilibrium relationship. Finally, the simplification of the autoregressive distributed lag equation proceeds according to a set of sequential statistical tests and the resulting equation is deemed satisfactory only when it successfully meets each of the six criteria given above. Hendry (1979, especially pp. 222–32) has labelled this modelling methodology the 'general to specific', which he contrasts with the more traditional 'specific to general'. It is claimed by advocates of the 'general to specific' approach that it makes the modelling decisions explicit; for example, McAleer *et al.* (1985) observed:

> many of the difficulties applied econometrics currently faces originate in the very poor attempts currently made to accurately describe the process whereby a model was selected, and to ascertain its adequacy... we proposed a three-stage approach to modeling [sic], involving the selection and subsequent simplification of a general model and a rigorous evaluation of any preferred model. Under the latter heading five ways of performing such an evaluation were distinguished [a re-grouping of the Hendry and Richard criteria cited above]. It may not be too fanciful to think of such criteria as a 'check list' to be applied when reviewing or performing applied work. Only if a model passes most items on the list should it be seriously considered as augmenting our knowledge (p. 306).

There is, thus, an almost mechanical purity surrounding the 'general to specific' simplification strategy (although it is to be noted from the McAleer *et al.* quotation that they only require the chosen model to pass 'most items on the list'). In practice, then, the intended purity of the procedure is contaminated, as Cuthbertson (1985) has observed:

> In practical applications of the ADL [autoregressive distributed lag] 'general to specific' methodology, the initial ADL equation is chosen to be as unrestricted as possible. However, with a limited data set the so-called unrestricted equation will usually contain some restrictions (for example potentially important variables omitted). After 'testing down', these restrictions may be released, for example, by adding 'new' variables as more degrees of freedom are then available. This destroys the purity of the testing down procedure .... (p. 268).

Although Cuthbertson does not give references to such practices, examples are not difficult to find. For instance, Davidson *et al.* (1978), having begun with a general ADL relationship between consumption expenditures and income, and having tested down to a preferred equation, then add two new regressors (one measuring the level of inflation and the other its rate of change). This is done in order to 'test' Deaton's (1977) hypothesis of the effect of inflation on consumption. As a check of the specification of the enlarged model, Davidson *et al.* proceed to estimate a 'new' general unrestricted equation relating consumption to *both* income and prices in autoregressive distributed lag form. The restrictions embodied in the equation used to examine Deaton's hypothesis are then tested against this 'new' general model and are found not to be rejected. Clearly, this is a procedure open to the objection that had the ADL model including prices been the starting point, then the finally chosen equation may not have resulted from the testing down procedure, *even though the restrictions embodied in it are not rejected.* Nothing in this relaxation of exclusion restrictions ensures that relaxation in other directions would also not be rejected against the general equation. This is precisely the sort of *ad hoc* method which Cuthbertson sees as contaminating the purity of 'general to specific' modelling.

The specification route proposed by Hendry seeks to correct the faults he perceives in the 'specific to general' (i.e. the 'traditional') method; however, there are certain problems with his suggested alternative, some of which are noted in Hendry (1979). One major problem which seems to have been the subject of very little attention concerns the implications of the two underlying assumptions, namely that economic time-series data reflect a disequilibrium process and that that process may be modelled by the use of autoregressive distributed lags.

The methods proposed by Hendry effectively assert that the simplest equation is an inappropriate starting point for empirical analysis. Thus, before any estimation is attempted, the equation is augmented by lags. However, the simplest model may well have shortcomings which are due, not to its dearth of lags, but to some other salient features which are misspecified, such as omitted variables. The addition of lags may actually contribute to the concealment of such misspecification, especially when the presence of multicollinearity ensures a similar information content of omitted variables and included lags. This possibility may be examined by the use of appropriate diagnostic tests; however, if one starts with the restricted equation then such tests are a natural part of the specification process, and if the equation is found wanting *then* it may be respecified by, for example, the addition of new variables or *possibly* lags of those already included; which route is to be taken would be determined by the utilization of economic theory (through examination of the auxiliary hypotheses). Furthermore, the presumption of the 'general to specific' method, that the data are generated by a disequilibrium process which may be proxied by lags, is not tested by those who advocate this method; rather it is taken as a fact of life (with reference made, typically, to the 'time-series nature' of the data). This recourse to a statement of faith stands in stark contrast to Hendry's own prescription for modelling, namely to 'test, test and test' (1980, p. 403). Indeed, were this *composite* assumption (namely that the data are generated by a disequilibrium process which may be proxied by lags) to be tested it would involve the specification of at least two models – one equilibrium and one disequilibrium – and the very test procedure would force the investigator to specify a disequilibrium model as an alternative to an equilibrium model. The former model would, ideally, not simply be based on the *ad hoc* method of adding lags, but would involve an *economic theory* of the optimal behaviour of economic agents out of equilibrium.[15]

SOME METHODOLOGICAL OBSERVATIONS

Advocates of the 'general to specific' strategy adopt a verificationist stance. However, the use of lags does not, typically, reflect any explicit economic theory[16] and hence any 'test' of theory within this framework must make recourse to the implied 'long-run steady-state' relationships rather than use the estimated autoregressive distributed lag equation directly. There are several methodological objections to this approach. First, 'long-run dynamic equilibrium' is a concept which has no material, protocol counterpart; we are never in a position to observe either such an equilibrium or the conditions which would, if undisturbed, lead to such a position. Second, deductive theory very rarely addresses itself to long-run dynamic steady-state equilibrium and, therefore, can provide few predictions of how variables (whether they be expressed as levels or rates of change) enter such relationships. Third, and perhaps most important, if economic theory were to be developed explicitly within the context of dynamic growth then a methodologically sound way of proceeding would be to use such predictions as hypotheses, in principle capable of refutation, which could then be tested.

In contrast, the practice adopted by those who have estimated autoregressive distributed lag equations is to treat the implied steady states as a source of 'verifying evidence'. A particular example of this is to be found in Hendry (1980): having estimated a dynamic demand for money function and having computed the implied long-run dynamic equilibrium solution, he observed that the result 'is *consistent with the hypothesised demand schedule*' (p. 401, original emphasis); no attempt to *test* the hypothesized demand schedule is made. Another example may be found in Hendry (1983, p. 211) when, having estimated a dynamic consumption function and having derived the implied long-run dynamic steady-state equation he proceeded to interpret the equation in the light of the Life Cycle Hypothesis (LCH). Since that hypothesis is not presented *a priori* as a maintained hypothesis, the exercise cannot be seen as an attempt at falsification; rather Hendry merely observed that the resulting steady-state equation may be interpreted as *consistent* with the LCH, but without indicating what state(s) of the world (as viewed through this model) would be *inconsistent* with the LCH.

The use of econometric evidence as verification of theory is, in fact, an explicit criterion for the evaluation of models within this strategy (see Hendry and Richard (1983), cited above as the second criterion); this is repeated by McAleer *et al.* (1985) in their criticisms of Leamer. The use of empirical analysis in the attempt to refute economic hypotheses requires far more careful selection of the original 'general' model than is demonstrated by those who advocate 'general to specific' modelling. However, although the selection of the general model is seen by McAleer *et al.* as 'pivotal to the methodology advanced' (p. 299), no criteria are offered to direct the researcher towards appropriate methods of choice. Rather, they side-step the issue: 'Selection of a general model is a problem with all research methodologies' (p. 299). Not only does this view side-step the issue; it begs a most important question, for it presumes that a *general* model is the appropriate starting point for an econometric methodology.[17] Indeed, if applied research is to proceed within a falsificationist mould then it is precisely at the stage of equation specification that economic hypotheses, capable of refutation, are introduced. Although this may constitute 'a problem', it can only do so if the investigator has no more specific conceptualization of the 'model' than a simple list of candidate variables; a falsificationist attitude demands far more than this – specifically it demands refutable hypotheses.

The practice of modelling from 'general to specific' fails to utilize the predictions of theory. Theory is never put to any test; rather, certain theories are merely *observed to be consistent* with the empirically derived steady-state relationship (or, more often, just one theory is 'verified' in this way). This practice might be described as naive empiricism, or theory after measurement which is to be contrasted with measurement after theory. However, what we have here is not so much the development of theory after measurement but rather theory *in parallel* with measurement; [18] in modelling from 'general to specific' there is little explicit connection between observational and theoretical statements and thus the econometric exercise fails to discriminate between clearly stated competing hypotheses. Of applied econometrics, Blaug (1980) remarked:

> Empirical work that fails utterly to discriminate between competing explanations quickly degenerates into a sort of mindless instrumentalism and it is not too much to say that the bulk of empirical work in modern economics is guilty on that score (p. 257).

Unfortunately, it would appear that the current practices in modelling from 'general to specific' open themselves readily to this kind of telling objection.

If we are to attempt to bring 'general to specific' modelling within the framework of science it would be necessary to modify current practices. In particular, it is hard to defend the strategy against the charge of measurement without theory, a charge first put forward by Koopmans (1947) in his classic attack. This argument has been furthered by Blaug (1980, p. 257) where he quotes from Kenen (1975):

> We do not distinguish carefully enough between the *testing* of hypotheses and the estimation of structural relationships (p. xvi, original emphasis).

The argument has also been advanced by Courakis (1978) in the context of demand for money studies, yet it would appear one cannot overemphasize that model specification is all too often determined using statistical criteria, and is insufficiently grounded in economic theory.[19]

'General to specific' modelling starts with an intentionally overparameterized equation which is then simplified to a more parsimonious form on the basis of various statistical tests. In defence of this method, Mizon (1977) stated:

> Until such time as economic theory provides detailed information about the dynamic specification of models, applied econometricians must continue to solve these specification problems empirically (p. 117).

From a methodological point of view, it is worth noting the following. First, specifications which have only an empirical basis represent only measurement without theory and, in the absence of a precisely stated maintained hypothesis, contribute little. Indeed, it appears that since the length of the lags is determined first by what 'seems reasonable to consider' (Hendry and Mizon, 1978, p. 555) – in effect a circular statement – and then by the application of sequential statistical tests, the maintained hypothesis is insufficiently well defined for the purpose of formal examination. This procedure is a particular example of those which form the basis of Kenen's criticism noted above. Something of a methodological compromise may be reached, however, if the model is chosen on the basis of analysis of a limited data set, and an expanded data set is then used to test for the stability of the favoured model. Such a compromise, much practised in recent applied econometric work, is, nevertheless, still lacking a sound foundation in economic theory. Even though the weight of empirical evidence is enhanced by such a process, the practice is still vulnerable to the standard critique of induction – we have no idea whether we may expect such stability in the future, nor of what might cause it to disappear. Moreover, though the weight of empirical evidence is undoubtedly enhanced by the statistical procedure of failing to reject the hypothesis of stability, the evidence remains no more than statistical.

Most recently, Rose (1985) has attempted to apply the techniques of dynamic econometric modelling to the US demand for money. Although he appears to be an enthusiastic supporter of the method, Rose nevertheless concedes that:

> Despite its reasonable steady state properties, the accusation that (7) [the final equation chosen by Rose] was obtained by a sophisticated form of data mining is undoubtedly not wholly unjust (p. 447).

Also, Leamer (1985a), attacking the Hendry–Mizon–Richard proposals for model selection described them as 'a combination of backward and forward step-wise (better known as unwise) regression' (p. 312). The data-mining accusation is not new; Hendry (1983) remarked that the empirical procedure has sometimes been:

> referred to pejoratively as 'data mining'. However, 'from the fact that it is of no scientific or logical significance how a theory is arrived at it follows that no way is illegitimate' (Magee, 1982, p.32) (p. 198).

Magee's remark, called upon by Hendry to support his position, does not, in fact, offer *any* support for the 'general to specific' method. The empirically derived 'best equation' is not deserving of the label 'theory';

rather it represents the result of a particular estimation strategy which has proceeded in the absence of any clearly stated theory; it is certainly not a part of the hypothetico-deductive method by which theories are derived *a priori* and put to the test of falsification. Magee is correctly reporting Popper; Popper argued that a theory is a logical construct which, as developed, will involve falsifiable hypotheses. The original starting point of the theory is indeed irrelevant *but the falsification is crucial*. Hendry would appear to have confused the origin of the initial 'vision' with the scientific procedures of theory development and theory testing and this is suggestive of a fundamental misunderstanding of the philosophy of science. Further, Hendry's methodological stance would appear to distinguish between the specification of the 'data generation process' (DGP) and the testing of economic hypotheses, and to regard the latter as being of subordinate – if not, indeed, peripheral – interest. Thus Hendry (1979) stated:

> Until the model adequately characterises the data generation process, it seems rather pointless trying to test hypotheses of interest in economic theory (p. 226).

One objection to this stance is that the so-called 'data generation process' does not have an existence independent of economic behaviour; data are never approached without a 'hunch' about their pattern. Unfortunately, reluctance to recognize this leads to a situation in which the hypotheses are present in disguise and not directly tested. Hendry's own statement of his methodology is that:

> my own empirical 'research programme' has been to investigate modelling based on *minimal* assumptions about the intelligence of agents and the information available to them, with maximal reliance on data using 'economic theory' guidelines to restrict the class of model considered (1980, p. 402, original emphasis).

Superficially, this proposal seems equivalent to the use of *economic concepts* but not *economic theory* in the determination of the DGP; indeed, for those involved in general to specific modelling, theory only constrains the class of model considered in so far as it is used to indicate the set of variables under consideration. However, the meaning attached to economic concepts is particular to the economic theory of which they are a part; indeed, concepts are defined within the context of the theory. Inevitably then, the set of variables chosen is itself a composite hypothesis of economic theory and in all areas of economic analysis it is the specification of this set which is a major focus of theory development. To rule out some variables and to include others is precisely what is meant above by the appearance of economic hypotheses in disguise. The interesting questions of theory development are, therefore, side-stepped by concentrating on the DGP and seeking to identify it as if it were some statistical concept independent of economic behaviour. The 'three golden rules of econometrics' adopted by Hendry (1980, p. 403) are 'test, test and test'; unfortunately, he does not extend these rules to the economic hypotheses which are *implicit* in the foundation of any DGP. Indeed, this approach actually appears to *deny* any role to economic theory in the DGP. This is not a defensible position.

Moreover, any attempt to test economic theory within the constraints imposed by the chosen DGP would be conditional on the specific form of the DGP chosen: since the chosen empirical relationship is viewed as an adequate description of the data generation process, any economic hypothesis which is inconsistent with the DGP simply leads the investigator to search for an *ex post* rationalization of the empirically derived equation and this takes us back to the methodological position of the naive empiricist. Alternatively, any hypothesis which is found to be not inconsistent with the DGP merely provides evidence of 'verification'. Thus, having 'discovered' the DGP, the investigator must search for an economic hypothesis consistent with it. Such a position is logically uncomfortable *since a wide range of otherwise competing hypotheses may be consistent with a DGP* (which is precise only in its computational procedures). That this position of verificationism is far from uncommon amongst economists is no comfort.

In the recent work by Spanos (1986), an attempt has been made to develop some of the Hendry–Mizon–Richard concepts. Some discussion of this work is warranted, for it purports to offer a 'methodology' of econometrics. Unfortunately, much of Spanos's work is methodologically flawed, and it is the intention of what follows to highlight those flaws.

SPANOS'S CONTRIBUTIONS TO ECONOMETRICS

Spanos observes that the Box–Jenkins ARIMA models (which have no explicit economic content) proved superior on predictive grounds to large-scale macroeconomic models and that this prompted renewed interest in the issue of '*static theory versus dynamic time series data*' (1986, p. 15, original emphasis). Further, he observes that 'the conventional econometric approach of paying little attention to the time series features of economic data' (p. 15) was questioned. He then goes on:

> The first possible weakness of the textbook methodology is that the starting point of econometric modelling is some theory. . . . [this] presupposes that the only 'legitimate information' contained in the data chosen is what the theory allows. This presents the modeller with insurmountable difficulties at the statistical model specification stage when the data do not fit the 'straightjacket' [*sic*] chosen for them *without their nature being taken into consideration* (p. 17, 18, emphasis added).

Such a position seems open to challenge on at least four substantive grounds.

1. The apparent success of ARIMA models is often interpreted as providing a bench-mark against which to judge econometric models; however, this is not, strictly, legitimate. Since ARIMA models do not utilize the hypotheses of economics, but are merely statistical constructs empirically derived, they are open to the charge of naive empiricism; to judge them solely when they 'work' does not comprise an acceptable comparison with econometric models. Because econometric models take account of the underlying *economic* structure of the phenomenon in question, they will outperform ARIMA models in many circumstances. For example, consider a univariate ARIMA model of the UK inflation rate identified and estimated using monthly data, from 1966 to, say, the middle of 1972. Such a model would seriously underestimate the inflation observed in the period 1973 to 1976 since it takes no account of, for example, the influence of the exchange rate and the oil price (Sterling was floating from June 1972 and there were two major oil price shocks in 1973 and 1974). It is not unreasonable to assert that an econometric model taking account of these factors would be superior on predictive grounds.

    As a quite separate argument, it is to be noted that *predictive ability is not a decisive criterion unless the investigator takes the methodological decision to view predictive ability as decisive*. Predictive ability, beyond the sample used for estimation purposes, is *per se* open to criticisms of inductivism and provides little information. The 'failure' of a mechanical extrapolation (such as that from an ARIMA equation) does not indicate any particular next course of action, while the 'success' of a mechanical extrapolation is data-specific, cannot be generalized to other occasions and is devoid of any explanatory power (because we do not know why it 'works'). In contrast, examination of the predictive ability of a model arrived at through the methodological route of falsificationism does provide information. Specifically, if a model which has been deemed otherwise 'acceptable' fails to predict with 'sufficient' accuracy, then this is an indication of a problem and will serve to direct research energy to its 'solution' (which could, for example, be that the model is genuinely deficient in this respect or that it is simply not applicable to this circumstance because there has been some significant structural change in the underlying process). Note, however, that this use of prediction as a criterion of a model is only used *after* the model has been acceptably specified through the utilization of economic hypotheses, both main and auxiliary, within a falsificationist methodology.[20]

2. The so-called time-series properties of an economic time series *cannot be viewed as features which are independent of their economic content*. If a particular variable is observed to have a trend, for example, it ill behoves the *econometrician* to work with de-trended data and seek no *understanding* of this feature. 'Paying attention to the time-series features' seems to mean little more than describing them and identifying those features which cannot be identified as 'time-dependent'. As such, the procedure does not enquire into the source of such features, does not utilize any economic theory and, therefore, fails to further our understanding of economic phenomena.

3. It is extraordinary that in a section entitled 'A sketch of a methodology' it is suggested that a 'weakness' of the textbook approach (or indeed any approach) is the fact that it begins with 'some theory'. In the first place, no observation statement is independent of theory (although the theory may well be implicit, in disguise); indeed there is no simple dichotomy between theory and observation. Moreover, the very purpose of investigation is to further *understanding* and this can have no meaning in the absence of theory; description does not constitute understanding, though even a description is based on some (possibly implicit) theory regarding the variables chosen to form that description.

4. The remark regarding the 'nature' of data is related to the previous point; namely it presupposes that economic data have some features which can be modelled without reference to economic theory but with reference to other economic variables. This is an indirect reference to the DGP; this, and related issues, will be examined below.

Spanos makes use of the concept of the DGP (defined as 'the mechanism underlying the observable phenomena of interest' (p. 20)) and defines terms such as 'theory' ('a conceptual construct . . . which will enable us to seek explanations and predictions related to the actual DGP' (p. 20)), 'statistical model' ('a probabilistic formulation purporting to provide a generalised description of the actual DGP'(p. 21)) and 'empirical econometric model' ('a reformulation (reparameterisation/restriction) of a well-defined estimated statistical model in view of the estimable model which can be used for description, explanation or/and prediction'(p. 21)). Since all these concepts are related to the DGP, they are all suspect on the grounds that the DGP does not have any existence independent of theory, as explained above. For Spanos, theory has no explicit contribution to make to the specification of the DGP, and the 'econometric model' is no more than a special case of the 'statistical model' which itself is a 'generalised description of the DGP'. This suggests that we can start by making no reference to economic theory (except in so far as choosing the variables to consider), search for the DGP, expressed as a statistical model, and identify it through the application of statistical tests. Then, through reparameterization and the imposition of restrictions, we arrive at the econometric model. This approach to modelling is equivalent to a failure to state a main hypothesis (H) and to stating no auxiliary hypotheses (A_i); in fact, the process only seems to utilize auxiliary hypotheses which appear *implicitly* in the choice of variables to consider. Methodologically, therefore, this proposal amounts to a rejection of the falsificationist methodology, a retreat into verificationism and a move towards naive empiricism. On each of these grounds the proposal is to be regretted. Spanos, however, seems to be aware of the dangers of verificationism but, by misinterpreting both the textbook method and the nature of scientific endeavour, charges 'textbook econometrics' with being 'rooted in an outdated philosophy of science' (p. 661). This is a wholly unfair charge as the traditional method is more than capable of supporting a falsificationist strategy; that Spanos chooses to ignore this interpretation is something of a curiosum.

Perhaps even more curious is Spanos's statement that 'bridging the gap between the isolated system projected by a theory and the actual DGP giving rise to the observed data chosen is the econometrician's responsibility' (p. 664). Spanos's dependence on the construct of the DGP has the consequence that the tail (the DGP) is wagging the dog (econometric investigation)! To assign such a minimal and subordinate role to economic theory in formulating and testing models is wholly anti-scientific at one level, but at another it is quite delusory since *the very choice of variables represents a set of auxiliary, unstated, hypotheses.* Moreover, by calling upon Caldwell (1982) *as authority* in methodological discussion, Spanos seeks to give the impression that Caldwell's views are wholly accepted by the economic profession; unfortunately, for the position Spanos is seeking to defend, this is not the case.

Finally, Spanos concludes:

> A main feature of the new methodology is the broadening of the intended scope of econometrics. Econometric modelling is viewed not as the estimation of theoretical relationships nor as a procedure in establishing the 'trueness' of economic theories, but as an endeavour to understand observable economic phenomena of interest using observed data in conjunction with some underlying theory in the context of a statistical framework.

We find it impossible to discern a meaningful distinction between the estimation and testing of hypothesized economic relationships and the endeavour to understand observable economic phenomena.

CONCLUSION

This chapter has sought to show that modelling from 'general to specific' requires rather more careful interpretation than has typically been the case. In particular, dynamic estimating equations, purporting to represent disequilibrium behaviour, lack a sound theoretical basis, and thus are open to the charge of 'measurement without theory'. Salmon (1982, p. 615) has remarked: 'The interface between economic theory and applied econometrics is often one of uneasy compromise'; a purpose of this chapter has been to identify the nature of that methodological compromise within the framework of 'general to specific' modelling and to suggest a possible route by which such model selection techniques may be better integrated into economic method. Specifically, it is proposed that the difficulties associated with the current state of dynamic econometric modelling should provide an impetus for the provision of a well defined theoretical basis on which to erect the statistical analysis of economic phenomena. Economists must attempt to work their way forward to the point where economic theory *does* provide information about the dynamic specification of economic behaviour for, as Koopmans (1947) argued, the:

> utilisation of the concepts and hypotheses of economic theory as a part of the process of observation and measurement promises to be a shorter road . . . . to the understanding [of economic phenomena] (p. 162).

So we need better theory. But in the meantime let us recognize that there is no such thing as observation without some underlying hypotheses, however loosely formulated. All observation statements are:

> made in the language of some theory and will be as precise as the theoretical or conceptual framework that they utilise is precise [21] (Chalmers, 1980, p. 27).

But 'general to specific' modelling uses a theoretical framework which is insufficiently precise. Thus the 'inductively' based conclusions cannot be seen as making any significant contributions to our understanding of economic phenomena. The identification of the weaknesses of what is seen by many as 'current best practice' (i.e. 'general to specific' modelling) will, it is hoped, provide an impetus for the development of appropriate economic theory within the dynamic framework which is a focus of interest of such econometricians.

NOTES

1. See Chapter 4 for a description and assessment of 'traditional modelling'.
2. Leamer's work is discussed and assessed in Chapter 6.
3. The simple equation (1) is used in preference to a more general equation involving a constant term and several explanatory variables since this device is without loss of generality.
4. Typically, economic theory is no guide to the choice of m. A usual pragmatic choice with quarterly data is 5, thus allowing the final equation to include terms of the form $(1 - L)(1 - L^4)$.
5. These expressions are taken from Hendry (1979) p. 228.
6. The order of the criteria given here is not that of Hendry and Richard (1983), but follows that of Gilbert (1986) where the interested reader will find a most stimulating discussion of Hendry's econometric technology. The criteria given in the text are not, of course, exclusively directed towards the modelling of economic time series; however, the current chapter deals almost solely with their application in a time series context.
7. There is a problem with this definition. The term 'logically possible' is circular since, without theory, there is no independent standard.
8. Weak exogeneity refers to the stochastic independence of the regressors and the error term; it is a wholly different concept to that of an exogenous variable which is a variable whose magnitude is not determined within the model under consideration.
9. The criteria are not sufficient; for example, they dictate that the equation should be chosen according to a verificationist methodology. This point will be taken up in greater detail in the text. The criteria are not necessary either; it is not at all clear that one should require of a 'successful' theory that it is capable of explaining all previous results (whatever their status).
10. Thus Hendry (1979) felt it appropriate to observe that ADL modelling 'highlights how apparent "structural breaks" in simpler equations . . need reflect no more than dynamic mis-specification' (p. 240).

11.   The steady states are those implied by the estimated, simplified, autoregressive distributed lag equation when the independent variables are either fixed over time or grow at some constant rate. From a purely technical point of view they are the implied particular solutions to the difference equation under two specific assumptions about the independent variable; they are conceptual devices, having no material world counterpart.

12.   For details of the derivation, the interested reader is referred to Currie (1981); an alternative method is to substitute the explicit time path of the independent variable into equation (2) and to solve the resulting difference equation for both the homogeneous and the particular solutions. The general solution comprises the sum of the homogeneous and the particular solutions. The solutions given in equations (4) and (6) are the particular solutions which will be the steady states if and only if the relevant homogeneous solutions decay to zero. This will be the case if and only if all the roots of the auxiliary equation lie strictly within the unit circle. For stability, therefore, we require that all roots lie within the unit circle. If any root lies outside, then the steady state solutions will diverge away from the particular solutions without limit. If a root is exactly unity (i.e. $\phi_0 = 0$), then the steady state solution comprises the particular solution as given, plus some constant which is the coefficient on the unit root. The stability requirements are described in more detail in Darnell (1986). For further details of the solutions of difference equations see, for example, Yamane (1968).

13. μ is the conventionally defined 'mean lag'. It should also be noted that the long-run equilibrium relationships (equations (4) and (6)) only hold when the independent variable is on its own long-run path and all adjustment is complete. If the system is shocked once in equilibrium, these relationships indicate the new equilibrium positions, but *not* the transition paths. The latter may be derived and may be of use in assessing the finally chosen specification.

14.   Since the concept of the long run requires all adjustment to the equilibrium path to be complete, the start value of x is arbitrary, as is the measure of time itself.

15.   This is not to say that lags would not be utilized in such a specification; what is important is the motivation for the inclusion of lags. If lags are included as a representation of an economic hypothesis, capable in principle of refutation, then their inclusion has theoretical justification and is not merely an *ad hoc* specification.

16.   Salmon (1982) has attempted to provide some linkage between *ad hoc* short-run adjustment schemes and economic theory through error correction mechanisms and, although this development is at an early stage, it is a most welcome attempt to utilize economic theory to specify disequilibrium behaviour.

17.   What has been proposed in Chapter 4, regarding the rehabilitation of 'specific to general' modelling, demonstrates that this is not the case.

18.   We are grateful to Denis O'Brien for this point, and for his expression 'theory *in parallel* with measurement'.

19.   For an extended discussion of this point, see Stewart (1979), especially chapter 9.

20.   For a discussion of the general problems associated with prediction, see Stewart (1979), especially pp. 79-85 and pp. 203-5. For a discussion of the relationship between goodness of fit statistics and the predictive ability of hypotheses, see Mayer (1975).

21.   The theory dependence of observations, and hence the lack of a perfectly secure observational base, is a problem discussed in Chapter 2.

6. The Contributions of Leamer to Econometrics

In 1983, Edward E. Leamer provided a significant challenge to econometric practitioners with his provocatively titled *American Economic Review* paper 'Let's take the con out of econometrics'. Although this paper brought Leamer to the notice of the general economic readership, he has written extensively in the field of statistical inference for over 15 years.[1] Of particular importance is Leamer's text *Specification Searches: Ad Hoc Inference with Non-Experimental Data* (1978).

Leamer's stance is Bayesian and he argues that, because classical inferential techniques were developed for the analysis and interpretation of data generated within the experimental sciences, they are inappropriate for the analysis of economic data.[2] However, Leamer merely offers an argument in favour of the Bayesian position; he does not prescribe a formal Bayesian view, claiming only that Bayesian analysis offers useful insights.

Leamer's contributions are directed not only at the general issue concerning the (mis-) use of classical statistical techniques with non-experimental data, but also at the gulf which he believes exists between econometric theorists and econometric practitioners.[3] Regarding the gulf between theorists and practitioners, Leamer remarks:

> We comfortably divide ourselves into a celibate priesthood of statistical theorists, on the one hand, and a legion of inveterate sinner-data analysts, on the other. The priests are empowered to draw up lists of sins and are revered for the special talents they display. Sinners are not expected to avoid sins; they need only confess their errors openly (1978, p. vi).

This is an uncomfortable view, for Leamer effectively rejects 'traditional' econometric practices as the act of 'sinful' activity, while viewing the theoretical developments of the 'high priests' as having little (if any) relevance to practitioners. This particular view rests on his interpretation of what he has christened the 'Axiom of Correct Specification' which he believes is sufficient to warrant economists 'to discard the textbook version of classical inference' (*op. cit.*, p. 3). Leamer's Axiom states that:

a) The set of explanatory variables that are thought to determine (linearly) the dependent variable must be:

1. unique,
2. complete,
3. small in number, and
4. observable.

b) Other determinants of the dependent variable must have a probability distribution with at most a few unknown parameters.

c) All unknown parameters must be constant.
   (*op. cit.*, p. 4).

Leamer describes this Axiom as 'unacceptable', a conclusion which is based on the following argument:

> If this axiom were, in fact, accepted, we would find one equation estimated for each and every phenomenon, and we would have books that compiled these estimates published with the same scientific fanfare that accompanies estimates of the speed of light or the gravitational constant. Quite the contrary, we are literally deluged with regression equations, all offering to 'explain' the same event, and instead of a book of findings we have volumes of competing estimates (*op. cit.*, p. 4).

Leamer's view is that the economists' ignorance of exact specifications is the cause of 'specification searches' and that this 'represents an unambiguous rejection of the axiom of correct specification and literally pulls the foundation from under classical inference' (*op. cit.*, p. 4). While it is self-evident that search activity is an integral part of empirical analysis, this does not necessarily invalidate the use of all classical procedures. The nature of search activity, explained in Chapter 4 within the context of 'traditional econometric modelling', has itself not denied the axiom, but has, rather, proposed a particular iterative search procedure designed to identify that algebraic form of the economic theory in question which allows testing of the main hypothesis. The technical difficulty with this search procedure is that of 'pre-test bias' which denies the investigator the textbook interpretation of test statistics. Leamer's contribution is to present an alternative, largely Bayesian, route by which to address the inevitable search procedures of econometric analyses. Leamer's stated position is that search activity of itself

> completely invalidates the traditional models of inference, both Bayesian and classical. But the Bayesian approach is sufficiently flexible that, with suitable

alterations, specification searches can be made legitimate, or at least under-standable (*op. cit.*, p. 2).

Our view is that the classical approach is equally flexible in making search activity 'understandable' (see Chapter 4), and that model uncertainty can be incorporated into classical testing, albeit informally.

Leamer has identified six types of specifications search:[4]

Type of search	Designed to
Hypothesis testing	Choose a 'true model'
Interpretive	Interpret multidimensional evidence
Simplification	Construct a 'fruitful model'
Proxy	Find a quantitative facsimile
Data selection	Select a data set
Post-data model construction	Improve an existing model

To the extent that data analysis is designed to further our ability to discriminate between competing hypotheses and test hypotheses of inter-est, all econometric analysis involves some search activity. This follows from the fact that any hypothesis of interest may be translated into a number of different algebraic formulations,[5] and only a sub-set of those formulations admits statistical inference;[6] econometric analysis is an aid to our determining those formulations which allow testing of hypotheses and which, therefore, enable us to decide whether to reject a hypothesis or not.

Leamer offers a 'theory' of specification searches, and while he is able to offer specific methods which he describes as 'unambiguously superior to current procedures' (*op. cit.*, p. 16), the conditions required to justify those methods are sometimes so restrictive as to be inoperable. Moreover, like so many who seek to popularize a particular point of view, Leamer contrasts his 'solutions' with what he calls 'current practices' which are, themselves, something of a straw man. While it is agreed that there is great room for the improvement of current econometric practices, our view is that what is wrong with those practices is more a matter of detail rather than of principle. Leamer's view is quite the opposite, namely that the use of classical statistical procedures is inadequate and should be replaced with Bayesian procedures.

At its simplest level, a Bayesian approach to inference requires an explicit, consistent and complete statement of the syllogism which is used to deduce testable predictions regarding economic behaviour. In particular, rather than simply assume the truth of auxiliary hypotheses, a Bayesian requires that the investigator assign prior probabilities to the union of the auxiliary hypotheses. Leamer objects to a step-wise method of specification in which auxiliary hypotheses are modified *en route* to the final specification, and then the final formulation is treated *as if* it were the only equation which had been examined. This is, therefore, in one sense an objection to those inferential procedures which proceed as if the pre-test problem were non-existent. The Bayesian approach does offer a mechanistic rule by which to integrate model uncertainty with sampling uncertainty, but the technical requirements are that the investigator is able to formalize all model uncertainty into a well defined prior density function. To the extent that model uncertainty is fuzzy, this will not always be possible. Leamer's answer to this challenge is to explore the implications of many different specifications, and this has been articulated in his proposals of 'Extreme Bounds Analysis' (see, especially, Leamer, 1983; and Leamer and Leonard, 1983).

Within Leamer's taxonomy, perhaps the most important form of search is 'post-data model construction', or as it has been christened, 'Sherlock Holmes inference'; indeed, although Leamer has sought to identify six different types of search activity it is conceivable to view the other five types as sub-search activity to post-data model construction. This follows from the motivations Leamer associates with each form of search: since the motivation for post-data model construction is 'to improve an existing model' this embraces all other motivations (see the table above). Methodologically, there are great similarities between Leamer's description of this kind of search activity and the kind of modifications to traditional econometric modelling which have been advanced in Chapter 4.

Leamer views Sherlock Holmes inference as the solution to a decision problem. As an example, suppose the economist is unsure of the role of variable Z in a regression, and initially proceeds on the assumption that Z's role is, in aggregate and on average, non-systematic. The regression of Y on X is performed (that is, Z is omitted initially), and as a consequence of inferences from this model, it is then decided to re-run the equation including Z.[7] The subtle difference between this proposal and the detective's method is that the economist must first have identified the potential role of Z, whereas the detective would have used data evidence to suggest the role of Z. This use of data, according to Leamer (*op. cit.*, p. 12), provides 'legitimate statistical inferences'. Methodologically, therefore, Leamer's major form of search is not at all different from our proposed method of traditional modelling: both require that the modifications to an equation after the initial data analysis are based on economic theory, and both require that the auxiliary hypotheses, necessary for hypothesis testing, are well specified before any regression is run. However, there is one aspect of Leamer's description of post-data model construction which demands comment.

Leamer states that the:

> Bayesian approach encourages more careful formulation of the model space, and to the extent that this is the right direction for the profession to move, the approach seems desirable. But Sherlock warns us against excessive theoretical developments before seeing the facts. The process of assigning probabilities to models tends to make the researcher believe and cling to his original set of hypotheses. This straitjackets his Sherlock Holmes instincts, and he may ignore important evidence simply because the relevant hypothesis is outside his immediate field of vision (*op. cit.*, p. 16).

The problem with this description is that it appears to suggest that 'facts' can be viewed in the absence of 'theory'; this is a view which we deny – all observation statements are made in the language of some theory[8] and in that sense all 'empirical facts' will 'straitjacket' inference simply because those 'facts' are stated with respect to a particular theoretical framework. The suggestion that 'facts can speak for themselves' in prompting the investigator to consider hypotheses which were not under initial consideration is not a tenable position; however, to suggest that empirical observations can lead the investigator to reconsider the initial treatment of auxiliary hypotheses is a quite different matter, and one which is methodologically sound.

Leamer's contributions are presented in more detail in the remainder of this chapter. While we have some criticisms of some of the details of his work, the spirit in which they are offered is to be welcomed, in particular, his view that 'The myth that inference with non-experimental data (or any data) could be judgment-free creates an insidious and a counter-productive goal' (*op. cit.*, p. 3).

LEAMER'S CONTRIBUTION

Leamer's contributions to econometrics are two-fold: an attempt to offer a theory of search behaviour and a novel method of reporting regression results. In fact, Leamer has presented not a theory of search but, by distinguishing various kinds of search activity, has provided an exercise in taxonomy. This has intrinsic value in identifying the nature of search; in offering some possible motivations for search; and in attempting to offer some justification for such practices. Additionally, Leamer has attempted to distinguish good search behaviour from bad. However, Leamer makes no explicit recognition of the methodological interpretation of the 'text-book' approach which we have offered in Chapter 4. In presenting Leamer's contributions, it is convenient to focus on the six motivations for specification search identified by him and then to examine the reporting strategy of Extreme Bounds Analysis.

SIX MOTIVATIONS FOR SPECIFICATION SEARCH

Leamer has identified six motivations for specification searches: hypothesis testing; interpretation; simplification; proximation; data selection and post-data model construction (also called Sherlock Holmes's inference).[9]

1. Hypothesis Testing Search

An hypothesis testing search concerns the estimation of a model which has been constrained according to some theory;[10] an example would be the estimation of a Cobb–Douglas production function subject to the constraint of constant returns to scale. Within a hypothesis testing search the theoretical constraint is tested using the usual statistical tools (i.e. 't' or 'F' tests). Leamer's label, therefore, refers *inter alia* to those occasions when a hypothesis in question defines simple constraints which, when imposed on a more general model, lead to nested specifications. Of course, within the familiar classical approach, it is well known that hypotheses expressed as simple linear constraints on the parameters may be tested using an 'F-test'.

It is not obvious that Leamer's terminology has added anything. What Leamer *has* added to our understanding of such procedures concerns the *appropriate* significance level of such tests. Additionally, Leamer discusses non-nested test procedures within a Bayesian framework and he offers some prescriptions regarding the integration of *model uncertainty* with *parameter uncertainty*.

Leamer observes that classical hypothesis testing at a fixed level of significance is a poor way of summarizing the evidence in favour of, or against, a hypothesis. Taking a Bayesian point of view, hypotheses are tested with respect to each other by computing the *Bayes factor* which relates the *prior and posterior odds* ratio. Leamer shows that when the investigator has no *a priori* favourite, the Bayes factor is determined in part by the sample size. A Bayesian prefers that model favoured by the Bayes factor, and in the case given above, this clearly is determined partially by the sample size; thus a Bayesian explicitly takes account of sample size in making decisions regarding the weight of evidence. The example given by Leamer demonstrates that within this class of prior, a Bayesian requires much larger 'F-values' than a classicist operating at the conventional 5 per cent level before rejecting a particular hypothesis in favour of the alternative. This leads Leamer to conclude that the conventional testing should be carried out with significance levels which are decreasing functions of sample size.[11] This point is also ably argued by McCloskey (1985a, 1985b).

The problem of non-nested hypothesis testing, the source of a voluminous literature within a classical framework, is dismissed as a problem by Leamer: he observes simply that the posterior odds are always given by the prior odds times the Bayes factor, *whatever the structure of the hypotheses*. Of course, the posterior odds rely on the prior odds chosen, and here the subjectivity and personal nature of Bayesian analysis is made explicit.

Within a Bayesian framework, the application of the rule of conditional probability provides a formula for incorporating model uncertainty with parameter uncertainty; the classical approach has no formal analogue. Inevitably, the Bayesian approach requires a formalization of the investigator's (subjective) prior 'probabilities' associated with the competing hypotheses and thus makes explicit the priors involved. Since classical analysis typically involves the use of ill-defined, implicit, priors it may be argued that it is healthier to have their role made explicit. This may, however, be interpreted simply as a call for classical analysts to be more careful in model specification by making the auxiliary hypotheses explicit.

A non-trivial problem with Bayesian hypothesis testing is the need to formalize the investigator's prior 'probabilities' of the competing hypotheses. The posterior odds favour hypothesis i so long as the Bayes factor exceeds the reciprocal of the prior odds in favour of hypothesis i; in this way, therefore, the setting of the prior odds actually determines the strength of the data evidence which is required to overturn the *a priori* view. Alternatively, a Bayesian may say that the data evidence favours one hypothesis relative to another depending on whether or not the Bayes factor exceeds unity (i.e. whether or not the data evidence enhances or reduces the prior odds, independent of the posterior odds *per se*).

A number of complicated issues arise because the Bayes factor is not a wholly data dependent term. In fact, this term depends on the data *and* on the prior probabilities of the parameters associated with each hypothesis; thus, in hypothesis testing, the Bayesian employs prior probabilities of the hypotheses *per se*[12] and also of the parameters associated with each hypothesis. If we denote the parameters associated with hypothesis i as θ_i, and the associated prior by $f(\theta_i)$, then the Bayes factor depends on the data and on both $f(\theta_i)$ and $f(\theta_j)$. Utilizing notions of diffuse priors regarding the parameters θ_i and θ_j leads to serious problems: as Leamer demonstrates, diffuseness leads to the Bayes factor adopting any value between 0 and infinity! (see especially p. 111). A route out of this difficulty (though hardly a solution) is to use dominated priors, that is priors which are dominated by the sample information so that their influence becomes negligible. This leads to particular expressions for the Bayes factor, but such formulae may only be used when the sample information dominates the priors, and this may or may not be the case. Alternatively, one could utilize specific priors, but then we are back at the problem concerning their personal nature.

2. Interpretive Searches

Searches designed to facilitate the reporting of multidimensional evidence are labelled interpretive searches. Leamer's interest in such searches stems from his observation that *ad hoc* search procedures, designed to 'discover' acceptable 'final' models, employ *implicit* priors. These search procedures, which he criticizes, involve *contracting*, *expanding* and *non-sequential* searches. Leamer advocates the assessment of interpretive searches by asking the Bayesian question: 'does an interpretive search lead to a description of the uncertainty similar to a posterior distribution corresponding to some prior?' (p. 123). He observes that there are at least three ways of dealing with prior information:

1.   Since prior information is difficult to specify personally and may vary significantly from one person to another it should be ignored, and the reporting exercise should involve only a complete statement of the

sample likelihood function.

2. Because the likelihood function 'defies intelligible reporting' (p. 124) in high dimensions, Bayesian analysis should be used as a method for exploring the likelihood. Any difficulties with the personal nature of priors should be dealt with by performing a sensitivity analysis 'designed to characterize as generally as possible the mapping from prior to posterior distrlbution' (p. 124).
3. Because 1 above is not possible, an interpretive search is carried out which involves the fitting and refitting of many equations – 'one of perhaps hundreds of equations is selected and reported, often as if the others had never been estimated. The resulting estimate involves an unknown and perhaps undesirable mixture of prior and sample information' (p. 124).

A weakness of Leamer's discussion of interpretive searches is that it fails to recognize the methodologically sound interaction of deductive and inferential evidence offered in Chapter 2. Further, it is concerned only with point estimates rather than with interval estimates though, as he observes: 'This reflects the state of theoretical developments, not the importance of measures of dispersion' (p. 127).

Leamer argues that there are two sources of failure in interpretive searches: on the one hand it may be difficult to find a prior which makes a search seem reasonable, and on the other the output of an interpretive search is based upon some *implicit* prior information. Thus Leamer says: 'An interpretive search is . . . an inefficient way to use ill-defined, uncommunicable prior information' (p. 123). If Leamer were correct on this point, then such an investigator *could never proceed as a Bayesian since the priors are uncommunicable.* Indeed, Bayesians assume that all prior information can be written in the form of a prior probability distribution. Of course, a weakness of the Bayesian approach is that not all prior information is capable of translation into a well defined prior.

3. Simplification Searches

Whereas hypothesis testing and interpretive searches are designed to introduce uncertain prior information into data analysis, a simplification search arises from Leamer's observation that: 'The most general models appropriate for inference with non-experimental data are usually so cluttered with variables of an incidental nature that they are nearly impossible to comprehend directly. It is thus incumbent on the researcher to find vehicles for communication of his results' (p. 202). Simplification searches may be motivated by one of three issues: prediction, control or inference. These may be illustrated in the example of a variable thought to be determined by two sets of independent variables: $Y = Z\alpha + W\delta + u$; the three motivations ask, respectively – may we act as if δ were zero (i) if we want to predict Y (ii) if we want to control Y or (iii) if we wish to make inference about α?

In this discussion, Leamer draws the useful distinction between *statistical* significance and *economic* significance (which has also been the subject of examination by McCloskey (1985b)). Leamer's conclusions are, as he emphasizes, sensitive to the 'specific and often unwarranted assumption about the process that generates the explanatory variables. No simplification decision can be made without either an implicit or explicit study of the behaviour of the explanatory variables, and we hardly need say that an explicit study of their behaviour is highly desirable' (pp. 223–5). A particular disadvantage of simplification, whether or not pursued within a Bayesian framework, concerns the fact that for prediction, control and inference, the effects of excluded variables are compensated for in the coefficients on the included variables. Compensation may not be desirable because rather than asking if a variable may be neglected we are asking whether it may be compensated for; and compensation implies a link between the included and excluded variables and thus the resulting equation will fail to make adequate compensation if the historical correlations between the variables change. Leamer's conclusion is that the potential costs of simplification are sufficiently large as not to warrant simplification. However, all theoretical statements necessarily 'simplify' the phenomenon under investigation, and the Classical device of stating the auxiliary hypotheses explicitly will accommodate this facet of modelling.

4. Proxy Searches

Proxy searches[13] occur when measured variables are not directly analogous to their theoretical counterparts. At one level, this is related to the familiar problem of errors in variables, but at another it focuses on the choice of appropriate data. Thus if there are several empirical counterparts of a theoretical economic variable, the investigator must choose amongst them; the proxy typically chosen will be that which is, in terms of the investigator's own criteria, 'best'. One of the problems in a proxy search is that some data information is used up in the search procedure, and it is important to leave part of the data evidence to allow inferences of the model to be drawn. Leamer offers this, quite properly, as a separate category of search strategy, but it is neither particularly important nor informative; indeed, on the major issue of how to allocate the available evidence between making inferences of the theoretical parameters and making inferences of the parameters of the 'proxy' process, Leamer provides no answers.

5. Data-Selection Searches

Leamer observes that theoretical models rarely specify the particular set of observations which should be used in the estimation procedure; hence, in practice, investigators estimate coefficients with different subsets of data or different transformations of the data set and select the result which, according to their own criteria, appears as 'best'. This search procedure is a data-selection search. One of its characteristics is its data-specific nature: 'when the data evidence is partly spent to pick a data set, the regression equation that is finally selected to convey the data evidence at least overstates the precision of the evidence and likely distorts it as well [sic]' (p. 259). This criticism applies equally to proxy searches. His analysis covers such issues as non-spherical disturbances, outliers, non-normal errors, the pooling of disparate evidence and varying parameter models. Leamer's conclusion is that one should be wary of attaching too much precision to the results of such search procedures, and that it is improper to treat their results as if they had been produced in the absence of any search:[14] the search procedure itself generates uncertainty which should temper statements of precision regarding the parameters of interest.

6. Post-data Model Construction

Leamer (1974, 1978) identified a procedure which describes the process of searching for hypotheses which explain the data to hand; one of the problems to be confronted in such a search is 'how can we say whether the data favor or cast doubt on the new hypothesis, when the new hypothesis was, in fact, constructed to explain the data?' (1978, p. 283). Leamer calls such searches 'Sherlock Holmes' inference'[15] since that detective's method was to collect all the data together and then weave a plausible story around them. Of course, Sherlock Holmes always had a final piece of data denied to social scientists, namely a confession or admission of guilt; it is impossible to think of an analogy to a confession in data analysis and therefore our inferences are less than certain.[16]

The analysis concentrates on two sorts of problem: inference in pre-simplified models and inference within data-instigated models. A pre-simplified model is one which is a restricted form of the investigator's set of beliefs. There are two sorts of uncertainty in such models: sampling uncertainty and misspecification uncertainty. The important conclusion is that once the sampling uncertainty becomes small relative to the misspecification uncertainty, continued sampling is worthless. However, the measure of misspecification uncertainty is individualistic, captured in the investigator's own prior.

Of more importance is Leamer's analysis of data-instigated models, especially models which are expanded as a consequence of a preliminary estimation. Leamer asserts that the major error of inference arises because these inferential procedures effectively ignore the fact that earlier regression results have played a major part in producing the final equation. He provides a prescription which is designed to eliminate this 'problem'. There are a number of comments which are relevant.

All theories represent 'pre-simplified' models in the sense that some variables, thought *a priori* to have individual non-zero influences, are omitted. If all variables which had an influence were included, then the 'model' would be 'complete' but hardly a theory which, necessarily, is an abstraction from reality. In our description of the role of the auxiliary hypotheses in Chapter 4 we explicitly recognize the role of excluded variables, and choose to omit only those influences which can, in aggregate, be modelled as a white noise error. This is clearly an alternative to Leamer's representation, and is, in our opinion, a more fruitful way of approaching the difficult task of model specification and testing.

On the question of data-instigated models, Leamer says that the initial exclusion of some variables need not be viewed as representing a prior which sets each of their coefficients to zero. Rather it may be viewed as setting their net influence as approximately zero, on average (i.e. is effectively modelled by a zero mean stochastic term). His insistence that an expanded model should be analysed in conjunction with a set of priors consistent with those originally held is not immediately appealing: surely the original estimation, which leads the investigator to expand the model, has itself modified the original prior? According to this latter view, the interpretation of the final model uses new priors which assign non-zero means to the coefficients on the new variables. In this way, the researcher learns from the original estimation, and the resulting posterior is subsequently used as the prior in later estimation.

In summary, Leamer has provided a taxonomy of specification search: it is difficult to use and where it can be used, the full conditions are not met. Leamer's intention would seem to be to instil a strong caution in those who make inference with non-experimental data: most recently, he has written:

> A lengthy list of implicit and explicit assumptions is required to draw inferences from a data set. Substantial doubt about these assumptions is a characteristic of the analysis of non-experimental data . . . If this doubt is left unattended, it can cause serious doubt about the corresponding inferences (Leamer, 1987, p. 432).

Where Leamer is particularly prescriptive is in his work on Extreme Bounds Analysis.[17]

EXTREME BOUNDS ANALYSIS

Leamer proposes Extreme Bounds Analysis as a solution to the problems of reporting the results of empirical investigations. This method aims to improve the information content of the reporting of econometric investigations. Leamer advances a particular kind of research programme, one in which the researcher embraces those priors conceivably held by all potential investigators of the phenomenon in question.[18] This programme is given the label 'Extreme Bounds Analysis', and the objective is to examine the sensitivity of inferences to investigators' priors.

Different investigators hold different priors which dictate the set of explanatory variables to be used by any one individual; Leamer constructs that set of explanatory variables which is the union of all other such sets: in this way, the specific prior held by any one investigator concerns only a subset of these regressors. In this context, Leamer introduces the concepts of 'free' and 'doubtful' variables:[19] if a particular prior sets the role of some potential variables to zero then those associated variables are termed 'doubtful' with respect to that prior; the remaining variables are unconstrained and so are labelled 'free'. A 'doubtful' variable within one prior may not necessarily be 'doubtful' in other priors (and similarly for 'free' variables). For example, in Leamer's investigation of murder rates (Leamer, 1983), he sets up a number of different priors; one, labelled 'Right Winger', holds that deterrent variables are free, while all other potential variables are doubtful. At the other extreme lies the 'Crime of Passion' prior: only deterrent variables are doubtful while all other variables are free. In between these extremes lie priors which partition the variables differently. Leamer has sought to 'market' the idea of Extreme

Bounds Analysis (EBA) by encouraging the reader to imagine the estimation of a regression in which there exist a few variables which are certainties for inclusion and some other variables which the researcher is 'willing to entertain' (See Leamer's reply, 1985, to McAleer *et al.*, 1985 in the *AER*, 1985). It is important to note that the investigator carrying out an EBA does *not* hold any particular prior; indeed, the whole point of this exercise is to examine the sensitivity of inferences to changes in priors.[20]

In this conceptual framework the EBA investigator partitions the candidate regressors into 'free' and 'doubtful' according to the priors under consideration[21]; let us label these X and Z respectively. For any particular prior, the regression equation examined may be written as:

$$Y = \sum \beta_k X_k + \sum \theta_i Z_i ; \quad k = 1, -, K, i = 1, -, J \tag{1}$$

where the θ_i are arbitrary weights. Thus the variables X_k appear in each and every regression equation estimated according to this prior and the Z_i variables may or may not appear depending on the values assigned to the various θ_i. For example, a value of $\theta_i = 0$ implies that the variable Z_i is excluded from the regression. The EBA procedure reformulates the partition according to an alternative prior, and the regression, of the general form of equation (1), is rerun. For each parameter (whether associated with a 'free' or a 'doubtful' variable) there will be a minimum and a maximum estimate according to the prior used; Leamer's concept of 'fragility' is determined by the range of estimates obtained.

Equation (1) represents a set of relationships somewhat wider than that indicated by the prior: the prior sets the weights on the doubtful variables to zero, whereas Leamer's suggestion is to consider *all possible linear combinations* of doubtful variables, thus enlarging the scope of the sensitivity analysis.

Consider the example presented by Leamer and Leonard (1983); a researcher wishes to study the effects of education, age and IQ on earnings. A decision has to be made regarding the inclusion of variables designed to capture parental education and parental IQ. Leamer and Leonard observe that these variables would be controlled in an experimental environment yet, in the non-experimental environment, the only route is to include the variables in the equation as a substitute for experimental control. In this paper, they label such variables as 'doubtful'. This, it is to be noted, is a slightly different concept of 'doubtful' from that offered above.

This procedure provides a sensitivity analysis of the estimated coefficients on the free variables to the linear combination of doubtful variables;

however, the nature and value of the gain in understanding is less than clear. One of the most important maintained assumptions of EBA is that the error term is orthogonal to all the candidate regressors; thus, although an intention of EBA is to make specification uncertainty explicit, it ignores the possibility of error misspecification. Clearly, this is most useful as an expository device: however, it creates severe problems in the application of EBA. This is because there are values of θ which will imply non-white noise errors. At one level, the researcher is freed from the chores of diagnostic testing, yet the purpose of the exercise is to make inference from data. To this end the question must be asked: what happens if, with a particular θ, the error term is not white noise?

Such criticism does not detract from the great value of EBA: this lies in the *spirit* in which it is offered to the profession at large. It urges researchers to recognize explicitly the uncertainty they have about equation specification; and to provide a more honest statement of their activities at the computer terminal. However this is, once again, no more than an appeal for an explicit statement of the model building exercise, and especially for an explicit statement of the treatment of auxiliary hypotheses.

Within EBA the uncertainty about whether the effect of other variables should or should not be controlled can be explicitly recognized in the reporting of results and in this context an important term is introduced, that of 'focus variable'. Focus variables are those variables for which the researcher is keen to establish coefficient magnitudes (in the terminology of our description of 'traditional' econometric modelling, the focus variables are those contained within the main hypothesis, H). In the earnings example above, the three free variables were treated as focus variables. One can also think of examples in which just a subset of the free variables are focus variables; for example, the interest rate in a demand for money equation. In general, when the focus variables are free the objective of the econometric exercise is to establish a quantitative calculus.[22] The sensitivity analysis proposed by Leamer and Leonard will yield both a maximum and minimum value for the coefficient of each focus variable which is designed to inspire confidence in the nature of the result. For example, a 'large' range is interpreted as a *fragile inference*. The range obtained in this way is not to be confused with the range obtained from the construction of a confidence interval. The EBA range reflects model specification uncertainty in the construction of alternative point estimates; the range from a confidence interval reflects sampling uncertainty within a given specification.

CONCLUSION

Edward Leamer, who has been described as 'an unusual sort of econometrician' (Sims, 1979, p. 566), has written extensively in the field of statistical inference and he has persistently argued for a modification of the classical inferential method when working with non-experimental data. This chapter has offered a low-level exposition of Edward Leamer's rather technical contributions to the econometrics literature.

Many readers' acquaintance with his work will be limited to his 1983 paper, 'Let's take the con out of econometrics' and the paper by Cooley and LeRoy (1981) which adopts Leamer's method.[23] But Leamer has made many other contributions to applied econometric practices, in particular, his description of the ways in which investigators can be misled into placing too much faith in their inferences. Most importantly, he has invited practitioners to make explicit recognition of sources of model uncertainty; state *unambiguously* their search procedure; and introduce a little caution into their conclusions.

The spirit of Leamer's work is undeniably admirable and it is to be hoped that his work will have a lasting influence on data analysts in respect of the confidence with which they state their conclusions. Leamer's two distinct contributions to econometrics are, first, an attempt to offer a theory of search behaviour and second to suggest a method of reporting regression results. However, it has been shown that some of the methods espoused by Leamer are either difficult to implement or provide answers only in exceptionally specific circumstances. Most importantly, his proposals represent little more than a Bayesian formalization of the role of auxiliary hypotheses in model specification. In this sense Leamer has offered no more than that obtainable within the Classical framework. In particular, the starting point of Leamer's analysis is the Axiom of Correct Specification which, as argued above, merely highlights the phenomenon of pre-test bias. Just as Classical techniques are unable to quantify this phenomenon in practice, so Leamer's 'solutions' are not generally applicable. Nevertheless, his concentration upon the Axiom of Correct Specification has served to highlight the improper practice of simply ignoring the implications of a specification search for the interpretation of the 'final equation'. Perhaps there is little more to say than to emphasize the dictum expressed by Theil:

> Given the present state of the art, the most sensible procedure is to interpret confidence coefficients and significance limits liberally when confidence intervals and test statistics are computed from the final regression of a regression strategy (Theil, 1971, p. 605).

NOTES

1. See, for example, Leamer (1972, 1973, 1974, 1975a, 1975b and 1978).
2. Economic data are not typically, if ever, generated by an experimental framework; economists take their data from the real world, rather than from a well designed experiment, but this does not necessarily invalidate the use of classical statistical techniques. Recognizing that classical methods cannot be used indiscriminately within economics can lead one to modify and adapt those techniques (albeit informally); this view was explained in detail in Chapter 1.
3. In this connection he highlights the use of search procedures, so prevalent in econometric practice, but so little discussed by econometric theorists.
4. This table is taken from Leamer (1978) p. 6.
5. The translation of the simple economic hypothesis that '*ceteris paribus* Y is determined by X' into an equation requires the investigator to make a number of decisions: the investigator must, amongst other things, choose empirical counterparts of the variables, choose a data set, decide how to model the *ceteris paribus* clause and decide on a particular functional form. Any one of the original decisions may be in error, and the results of a specific regression equation may lead the investigator to re-examine those decisions and modify them accordingly.
6. Standard statistical testing is only possible when the error term in the regression has the qualities of being wholly non-systematic. The interpretation of the error term given in Chapter 1 and used in Chapter 4 means that only those equations which have residuals consistent with a wholly non-systematic error admit statistical testing of hypotheses of interest.
7. The decision to include Z may be a consequence of, for example, some diagnostic tests of the residuals or because the sign of the response of Y to X does not conform to the theoretical prediction.
8. See, for example, the comments made in Chapter 2.
9. Throughout this section of the chapter, all references are to Leamer (1978) unless otherwise indicated.
10. By definition all models are constrained but, as can be seen from the example in the text, this is a particular usage of 'constrained'.
11. This is an examination of the methodological norm of Type I errors.
12. These priors will, of course, generate the prior odds.
13. The definition given in the text is the typical case.
14. One might, pejoratively, consider this to be an example of mining potential data sets to find one that works.
15. To our knowledge, this term first appeared in Dhrymes *et al.* (1972) where it was attributed to an unnamed member of the set of authors, one of whom was Leamer.
16. The closest analogue to a 'confession' occurs within Monte Carlo experiments, when the 'true' structure of the model is known.
17. See especially Leamer and Leonard (1983). It is interesting to note that, in Pagan's appraisal of the work of Hendry, Leamer and Sims, the discussion of Leamer's approach was restricted to an appraisal of EBA. This is not surprising as Pagan's criteria of assessment were 'the provision of general research tools, the codification and transmission of principle, and the reporting of results'(Pagan, 1987, p. 19); for this it was necessary to focus on Leamer's prescriptive work.
18. This is, of course, an impossible aim: one could never take account of all conceivable points of view.
19. Leamer's work introduces the terminology of 'free' and 'doubtful', but the new terms are not unambiguously employed in the literature (see note 22). In what follows, therefore, we are using our own interpretations.

20.   In addition, one important maintained assumption of EBA is that the error is orthogonal to all the candidate regressors.

21.   The priors used in EBA are, then, such as to partition the candidate variables into 'free' and 'doubtful', which may be thought of as 'definite inclusion' and 'possible exclusion'.

22.   Free and focus variables have often been employed as if they are interchangeable, but this is not intended by Leamer. In his reply to McAleer *et al.*, he remarked 'It is often but not always the case that the free variables are also the focus variables' (Leamer, 1985, p. 309, fn. 2).

23.   The latter paper provoked a response from McAleer *et al.* (1985) which itself provoked a response from Leamer (1985a). One reason for any lack of familiarity with Leamer's work is the relative dearth of applications (see Pagan, 1987, p. 9).

7. Sims and Vector Autoregressions

Recent work by Sims on vector autoregressions was developed in a climate of dissatisfaction with the large-scale macroeconometric models built in the tradition of the Cowles Commission,[1] and at a time when knowledge of time-series models had spread amongst economists. Not only was the predictive performance of the large-scale models alleged to be poor but also their forecasts were alleged to be worse than those derived from time-series models.[2] Furthermore, the methods of identification and estimation of these simultaneous macroeconometric models were being questioned,[3] not least by Sims. Sims's influential paper, 'Macroeconomics and reality' (1980), developed the earlier argument (presented in Sargent and Sims, 1977) that researchers had made the 'unwarranted assumption' of too much *a priori* theory when building their models: Sims's objective was to present an alternative to the Cowles Commission approach taking into account the objections to that style of econometric analysis. He focused, therefore, on large-scale structural models of the economy formulated as systems of simultaneous equations with linear (often exclusion) restrictions; these restrictions are the standard means by which the identification problem is resolved.[4]

The importance of identification is that while it is generally possible to produce (estimable) reduced form equations from a simultaneous equation system, it may not always be possible to get estimates of the structural form parameters from the reduced form estimates and, sometimes, multiple structural estimates may arise. It should be remembered that the purpose of obtaining the reduced form equations is to exploit the *presumption* that in this formulation the right-hand side variables are uncorrelated with the residuals. From a methodological point of view this presumption is important as it is an auxiliary hypothesis of exogeneity necessary for estimation of the reduced form; from an investigator's perspective it provides a means of obtaining unbiased and consistent estimators of the reduced form parameters and, through them, consistent estimators of the structural parameters. The way in which restrictions have been applied is the key to the identification of a system of simultaneous equations; linear restrictions (exclusion restrictions) are one way of solving the identification problem. The precise role for economic theory in resolving the identification problem is therefore in the phrasing of the auxiliary hypotheses which dictate the specification of each equation in the system. These hypotheses dictate, *inter alia*, which variables are deemed salient and which are deemed non-salient; they therefore provide information regarding the restrictions relevant to each equation, and also regarding cross-equation restrictions. But notice that in meeting the objective of an identified system of equations the characteristics of the model specification have been dictated; for example, given an exactly identified equation, there is no scope for changing the specification by adding one of the exogenous variables which appears in other equations.

Debates about simultaneous equation systems have predominantly been concerned with the problem of over-identification and the criteria used in the selection of the set of included variables for the system as a whole: they can be traced back to the analysis of over-identified systems begun by Koopmans at the Cowles Commission in the 1940s. A major thrust of Sims (1980a) is to challenge this concern with over-identification and switch the focus to the problem of under-identification.[5] In order to appreciate Sims's challenge, more needs to be said about earlier work on the estimation of macroeconometric models.

THE COWLES COMMISSION

The construction of macroeconometric models is usually traced back to Tinbergen's (1939) work on business cycles, but the framework for the estimation of such models was largely created by the economic theorists and econometricians at the Cowles Commission in the 1940s and 1950s.[6] Jacob Marschak, research director of the Commission from January 1943, channelled resources into developing Tinbergen's work in the light of the statistical work on simultaneous equations systems carried out by Haavelmo and by Mann and Wald.[7] In this climate the Cowles Commission researchers developed an interrelated set of ideas and analytical tools for the estimation of macroeconometric models.

The purpose of the work was to make a statistical study of the causal explanations of macroeconomic phenomena. The Cowles Commission researchers viewed a structural equation system as an appropriate means of modelling the economic hypotheses that certain variables were jointly determined; the structural equations thus represented particular main hypotheses about economic behaviour (such as demand being negatively related to price) and economic theory defined the additional maintained restrictions (the auxiliary hypotheses) on the system in order to provide identified equations. In these ways the role of economic theory was made explicit: decisions regarding the endogenous variables to be examined and their determinants were based on the considerations of economic theory; moreover, the decisions regarding which variables were deemed *endogenous* and which *exogenous* played the role of auxiliary hypotheses, as did the restrictions on each equation's specification.[8] The main hypotheses of interest consisted of predictions regarding the structural parameters and in particular their signs. The spirit was one of verification. The ultimate belief (hope) was that textbook economic theory could be verified and estimated using relatively simple statistical techniques and could then be used to provide a basis for advising policy makers. Koopmans presented the view in a 1945 conference paper:

> The study of an equation system derives its sense from the postulate that there exists one and only one representation[9] in which each equation corresponds to a specific law of behavior (attributed to a specified group of economic agents) .... Any discussion of the effects of changes in economic structure, whether brought about by trends or policies, is best put in terms of changes in structural equations. For these are the elements that can, at least in theory, be changed one by one, independently. For this reason it is important that the system be recognizable as structural equations (quoted in Epstein, 1987, p. 65).

A major step in the Cowles Commission development was the publication, in 1950, of the Cowles Commission Monograph No. 10 in which Koopmans introduced exogenous variables to the Mann and Wald framework. This extension of Mann and Wald was to use economic theory to suggest exogenous variables to determine structure. This development offered a solution to the identification problem and it provided the means to represent the direct instruments of economic policy. (For these purposes exogenous variables were viewed as the independent variables in a classical scientific experiment.) Within the simultaneous equation framework, Koopmans analysed exogeneity for its statistical implications.

Koopmans (1950) identified two possible cases of exogeneity: one dealt with 'variables which influence the remaining (endogenous) variables but are not influenced thereby' and 'the second case generalized what Koopmans called predetermined variables' (Epstein, 1987, p. 172). Koopmans specifically named the first case as the 'causal principle', in the spirit of an experimental set-up. These variables were readily interpretable given Koopmans's examples of natural phenomena such as temperature and rainfall. In this context it is not difficult to accord with the 'strict' exogeneity requirement that a current exogenous variable should not be determined by any present or past values of the endogenous variables. However, this definition limits the number of economic factors that would readily be considered exogenous in a macroeconomic model: the limitations arise from the use of auxiliary hypotheses which have dictated which 'exogenous' variables are salient and which are not. Only salient exogenous variables have a role to play in identification; in many cases the auxiliary hypotheses determine too few exogenous variables for the purposes of identification. Koopmans's predetermined variables were therefore a welcome (and much needed) additional route towards gaining identification.[10]

Exogeneity is essential in this simultaneous equations approach because it provides a conceptual basis for understanding economic data as the result of experiments. Changes in exogenous variables could be thought of as shocks to the economic system and the induced changes could be predicted. Indeed, the appearance of the Cowles Monograph No. 10 prompted many discussions in the early 1950s on the interpretation of cause and effect within a multi-equation econometric model. Nearly all this work attempted to find a parallel to the stimulus–response structure of a conventional laboratory experiment.

Key features of the Cowles Commission approach to model specification are: restrictions from economic theory, presumptions about the direction of causation between economic variables and the property of exogeneity. The issues of causality and exogeneity are defined as equivalent given that, in the Cowles method, the data are assumed to have been generated by a system of simultaneous equations in which there are two sets of variables: exogenous and endogenous. With this endogenous/exogenous dichotomy, causation is defined to run from the exogenous variables to the endogenous variables. The direction of causation and the property of exogeneity are taken as given *a priori* and are untestable.[11]

This Cowles Commission approach forms the basis of the textbook presentation of macroeconometric model building; for example, most students of applied econometrics will be familiar with the Klein (1950) model of three behavioural equations and three identities (estimated by FIML, LIML and OLS). Klein built his first models at the Cowles Commission in the mid-1940s and went on to develop the Klein–Goldberger (1955) model, the first model to be used for regular *ex ante* forecasting purposes.[12] The use of macroeconometric models for forecasting was an important development, not least because it was responsible for shifting the focus of research: the demands made of a forecasting model are such that regular[13] updating of the models required the reallocation of research effort away from the 'basic' research of developing economic theory and developing statistically efficient methods for the estimation of the structural parameters of an *a priori* specified system of simultaneous stochastic equations. Certainly, into the 1970s, many models were enjoying commercial success (for example Data Resources Inc., Wharton Econometric Forecasting Associates and Chase Econometrics) and energies were largely directed towards the more practical needs of updating the models. Yet the 1970s was also a decade in which macroeconometric models were subjected to criticism on several grounds.

OBJECTIONS TO THE COWLES COMMISSION METHOD

One critical thrust relates to the adoption of rational expectations: if economic agents are postulated to form rational expectations based on an understanding of the processes which generate variables in the model (including government policy) then there are serious doubts about the invariance of the 'structural' parameters in macroeconometric models when government policy changes.[14] This line of argument led to the well known Lucas critique[15] in which it was argued that there is no reason to believe that the 'structure' of economic relationships remains invariant under a policy intervention, thus striking at the heart of the structural equation models.

One response to this criticism has been to construct macroeconometric models in which the 'expectations' and the 'forecasts' generated by the model are consistent. This is achieved by imposing cross-equation parametric restrictions, but problems of identification and estimation of these 'consistent' rational expectations models remain.[16] Sims's (1980a) response is in some ways more radical for he rejects the whole Cowles Commission style of achieving identification. Moreover, he expresses unease about *a priori* restrictions on lag lengths employed for the identification of rational expectations models.[17] Specifically, Sims, as an act of faith, asserts that all salient variables are to be included in *all* structural equations and therefore denies that *a priori* theory can yield the necessary restrictions for identification of structural models: this is *not* a testable assertion since the structural form is *not* estimable. Further, he argues that structural identification is not needed for forecasting and policy analysis.[18]

The view that economic theory cannot be relied on for identification is not new (see Liu, 1960). The argument runs as follows. Econometric models abstract from the real world by limiting the number of variables under consideration. There are always relevant variables which have been excluded both from the model as a whole and from each individual equation; however, identification through exclusion restrictions requires that *some* exogenous variables appear only in some equations, not all. A reluctance to appeal to economic theory to provide such exclusion restrictions denies identification. Further, virtually all variables appearing in econometric models are endogenous so that the models are generally underidentified.[19] Sims's replacement of *ad hoc* expectations formation with rational expectations, thus endogenizing more variables, is an extension of this line of thinking. This implies yet further difficulties for identification – importantly, there is no transformation of reduced forms into structural equations. This point is developed below.

VAR: WHAT IS IT ABOUT?

Sims's 'structural model' takes the form:

$$By_t + \sum_{j=1}^{P} \Gamma_j y_{t-j} = u_t$$

where y_t is an (N x 1) vector of all the current variables included in the model; the B's and Γ_j's are (N x N) matrices. In the model there are no exogenous variables, only predetermined variables. This style of modelling is a consequence of *presuming* that no variables are exogenous (for whatever reason). Further, it is assumed that no economic theory can be used to set elements of the structural form matrices to zero; thus this approach proceeds from the assumption that B and all the Γ_j are full (that is, not sparse) matrices. Clearly, were the implications of a specific economic theory imposed on this model, this would provide restrictions on the structure.[20] However, Sims's style is the antithesis of this familiar practice, choosing to model economic behaviour on the basis of no particular economic theory. It is in this sense that his work has been labelled 'atheoretical'.[21]

For Sims then, many identifying restrictions in macroeconomic models are deemed to be 'incredible', by which he means both that the presumption that some variables are exogenous is not innocuous and that, setting some structural form parameters to zero is, equally, not innocuous. In his view, the implication for econometric modelling is simple: the practice of excluding variables should be resisted – all variables should be deemed endogenous and should appear in all structural form equations. With no prior information as to lag lengths, only a set of equations with identical lags for all variables can be estimated. He called this alternative style of econometrics a 'vector autoregression' or VAR.[22]

In sharp contrast to the Cowles Commission approach, no theoretical restrictions are imposed in the estimation of vector autoregressive (VAR) models but some pragmatic restrictions (notably on lag lengths) are imposed. Sims argues that in principle all equations in a simultaneous system should have the same right-hand side variables in order to capture all possible forms of interaction among variables. In particular each variable in a VAR reduced form model is regressed on lagged values of itself and lagged values of all other variables in the model. For example an extremely simple two variable VAR is, in its reduced form:

$$\text{Income} = a \ (\text{Money supply})_{-1} + b \ (\text{Income})_{-1} + e_1$$
$$\text{Money Supply} = c \ (\text{Money supply})_{-1} + d \ (\text{Income})_{-1} + e_2$$

Here both the money supply and income are treated symmetrically, each is determined by its own lagged value and the lagged value of another variable thus avoiding any controversial theoretical restriction like exogeneity of the money supply. This is the essence of the VAR approach although a typical VAR model would include more variables and longer lags and as many equations as variables.

The VAR models are thought to provide a straightforward method of producing forecasts that do not constrain how their variables affect one another but importantly this approach is not free of restrictions. In practice, the size of VAR models is limited by the fact that each variable including lags appears in each equation yet estimation requires sufficient degrees of freedom. The modeller must therefore restrict the number of variables and the lengths of the lags used.[23] This restrictive feature is highlighted in comparisons of the forecasting performance of VAR models with large structural models. For example, Webb (1984) compares the forecasting performance of a five-variable, six lags VAR model with a structural model containing several hundred variables.[24]

THE VAR METHOD

Setting up and using a VAR model is a step-wise procedure which Pagan (1987, pp. 15–16) summarizes as follows:

I   Transform the data to such a form that a VAR can be fitted to it.
II   Choose as large a value of p (the lag length) and as large a dimension of (y_t) as is compatible with the size of data set available and then fit the resulting VAR.
III   Try to simplify the VAR by reducing p or by imposing some arbitrary 'smoothness' restrictions upon the coefficients.
IV   Address the question of interest using the orthogonalized innovations representation (explained more fully below).

The transformations in the first step are attempts to obtain stationary data series, that is series which are generated by a stochastic process which is invariant to time. The transformations are required because VAR modelling utilizes a set of techniques developed for the analysis of stationary time series yet most economic time series, when viewed as univariate time series, are typically not stationary. The VAR reduced form model can be written:

$$y_t = \sum_{j=1}^{p} A_j \, y_{t-j} + e_t$$

where y_t is an ($N \times 1$) vector of all the current values of the variables included in the model that represents a stationary stochastic process; the A_j's are ($N \times N$) matrices and the ($N \times 1$) stochastic error process e_t satisfies the orthogonality conditions; p is the lag length. Every variable in the ($N \times 1$) vector y_t has two components – its best linear predictor based on past values of all included variables and its linearly unpredictable 'innovation', e_t.

In steps I and II, prior information is only used to guide the selection of variables in the set y and to set the lag length p.[25] Step III requires some judgement on the trade-off between obtaining a general model and having sufficient degrees of freedom for estimation purposes, i.e. the inefficiency associated with over-parameterization must be balanced against the bias associated with a parsimonious parameterization.

Step IV requires some manipulation of the VAR model and has been the subject of much criticism (see particularly Cooley and LeRoy, 1985). The intended use of the VAR model is crucial here: there are two broad uses

–forecasting and policy analysis. Forecasts can be generated recursively from:

$$E_t (y_{t+1}) = \sum_{j=1}^{p} A_j \, y_{t+1-j}$$

$$E_t (y_{t+2}) = A_1 E_t (y_{t+1}) + \sum_{j=2}^{p} A_j \, y_{t+2-j}$$

and so on . . .

To use vector autoregressions for policy analysis it should first be understood that policy is interpreted narrowly to mean the addition of a known innovation shock to the model.[26] The VAR models are driven by stochastic shocks and the intention is to trace out the reaction of the system to a random shock. Thus, writing the moving average representation of the model:

$$y_t = \Sigma D_j \, e_{t-j} \quad D_0 = I$$

where the D_j are $(N \times N)$ matrices; and recalling that $e_t = y_t - E_{t-1} (y_t)$, it is possible to trace out the likely effects of unexpected shocks to the ith variable y_{it} on subsequent values of all the variables. This is all done under the unstated assumption that the behaviour of the system is not sensitive to the underlying economic origin or nature of the shock. The response of the whole system is then traced out, through simulation, by experimenting with different combinations of shocks. Importantly the vector autoregression model cannot be used to evaluate the effects of policy interventions in the form of changes in the feedback rule governing a monetary or fiscal policy variable. The reason is that if an equation of the VAR model describes an authority's feedback rule, then any change in the feedback rule will, in general, have implications for other equations in the model (that is, there are cross-equation restrictions).[27]

Thus, in the VAR model:

$$y_t - A_1 y_{t-1} - A_2 y_{t-2} - \ldots - A_p y_{t-p} = e_t$$

setting all $e_s = 0$, $s < t$ and $y_{t-i} = 0$, $i > 0$, the response of the y_t vector can be traced out over time through the innovations e_s, $s \geq t$. This is a period by period 'simulation' which can be carried out indefinitely to plot the response of the vector autoregression to a one-time only, or a persistent shock.[28] However this procedure may be misleading if any of the innovation terms are not wholly non-systematic but are contemporaneously correlated. For example, consider a simple two-variable, one-lag VAR reduced form model:

$$m_t = a_1 m_{t-1} + a_2 y_{t-1} + e_{mt} \tag{1}$$

$$y_t = b_1 m_{t-1} + b_2 y_{t-1} + e_{yt} \tag{2}$$

where m = money supply; and y = income, and in which it is known that the innovation terms are correlated. Let the error term e_{yt} be decomposed into (i) a portion explained by the other error term, e_{mt}, and (ii) a remaining independent portion. That is:

$$e_{yt} = \alpha e_{mt} + u_{yt}$$

Now the dynamic response of y to a unit shock in e_{mt} will be '$\alpha \Delta m$ in the first period' and '$(b_1 + b_2 \alpha) \Delta m$ in the second period'. This is to be compared with an inferred 'no impact on y in the first period' and '$b_1 \Delta m$ in the second period' when there is no correlation between the error terms (i.e. when $\alpha = 0$).

The mechanism used by VAR modellers to avoid making such misleading inferences is to transform the vector autoregression so that the transformed innovation vector has a scalar variance covariance matrix. In general, a convenient way to remove any contemporaneous correlation among series innovations is to apply a Choleski decomposition to the untransformed variance covariance matrix. This means that the VAR is transformed to:

$$Gy_t = GA_1 y_{t-1} + GA_2 y_{t-2} + \ldots GA_j y_{t-j} + Ge_t$$

where $G = H^{-1}$ and H is the Choleski decomposition of the untransformed model.

Notice that the Choleski decomposition has set up a 'Wold causal chain' among the current elements of the y vector. That is, y^1_t (the first component of the y vector at time t) has no other current period y^i_t in its AR representation; y^2_t has current y^1_t, but no other current values, in its AR representation and so on. Thus the causal chain in the current period runs from y^1_t to y^2_t. Importantly, this causal chain is arbitrary and any ordering of the variables could be used. This is fully acknowledged by Sims when he explains this procedure for his six-variable VAR model:

The residuals are correlated across equations. In order to be able to see the distinct patterns of movement the system may display [in response to a 'shock'] it is therefore useful to transform them to orthogonal form. There is no unique best way to do this. What I have done is to triangularize the system, with variables ordered as M, Y, U, W, P, PM . . . . [then] the M innovation is assumed to disturb all other variables of the system instantly, according to the strength of the contemporaneous correlation of other residuals with the M residual, while the PM residual is only allowed to affect the PM variable in the initial period (Sims, 1980a, p. 21).

The six variables can be ordered in 720 different ways in constructing a Wold form. To limit the choice, VAR modellers advocate the need to establish the direction of causation between variables in the system. The direction of causation is determined on the basis of causality tests[29] which, according to practitioners of VAR, allow one to determine whether, for example, *m* causes *y* or vice versa. Following the causality tests the variables in the system are ordered so that an error term in any equation will only affect error terms below it in the ranking. This ordering in variables is called a triangularization and amounts to admitting current variables into the list of regressors. In general therefore each equation in a VAR system (bar the first one) will include the current values of the dependent variable from each previous equation in the ordering, along with lagged values of all variables and current innovations in the dependent variable.[30]

In summary, estimation and analysis of vector autoregressive models normally commence with OLS estimation of an autoregressive system of equations such as (1), (2).[31] Then, some ordering of the variables is made which orthogonalizes the errors. As stated above, it is proposed that this takes the form of a series of causality tests between variables in order to determine some 'causal chain' in the system under consideration. However this is not always the case: for example Sims (1980a) orders the six variables in his model on the basis of his *a priori* beliefs, that is without reference to explicit causality tests. Following orthogonalization, the system's response to typical random shocks is then considered. This is done by simulating the response at $t = 0$ of the orthogonalized model to an innovation of one standard deviation in each equation of the system (individually not simultaneously).

APPLICATIONS OF VAR

The VAR approach has been applied in various contexts, most overtly as a naive forecasting tool and as a tool for policy analysis. Examples of the former are Sims (1982, 1986) and Doan, Litterman and Sims (1984); for examples of the latter, see Sims (1980a, 1982).[32] In addition, VAR models can be used for causality testing[33]; for example Granger's (1969) proposed test for causality is actually a two-variable VAR. Given this use, VAR models can be used to test theories which imply that one variable of the system should fail to Granger-cause another. One example (of five given by Cooley and LeRoy, 1985, p. 287–8) is the use of VAR to test capital market efficiency: if no variable in the information set, I, Granger-causes the rate of return on a security, r, then the expected value of r, given the information set I, is equal to a constant, i.e. the market is efficient. Moreover, the VAR models can be used to generate stylized facts about causal orderings using these as a process of hypothesis seeking. Subsequently, theorists seek to explain the empirical results – an example is Ashenfelter and Card (1982).

CRITICISMS OF VAR

Existing criticisms of VAR models have placed much emphasis on the transformations undertaken to yield causal chains. However, other aspects of specification have also been criticized together with the use of vector autoregressions for causal inference. First, it should be recalled that VAR modelling requires all variables to be stationary and therefore at the outset the data are transformed. However, transforming the data series is neither easy nor without risk of being misleading. See for example Plosser and Schwert (1978) who show that the frequently used method of differencing can be over-utilized with misleading results. Also Pagan (1987) criticizes Doan *et al.* (1984) for claiming that the inclusion of time trends in each equation of the VAR (on data series which follow a random walk) will be sufficient to induce stationarity; they may not be.

Second, the selection of the set of included variables is an important source of concern about VAR models. For example, conclusions about major macroeconomic issues, like the role of money in the economy, are found to be sensitive to the inclusion of an additional variable in the model. In particular, Sims (1982) notes that 'the estimated [monetarist] response of the system to a disturbance in money stock ... disappears in systems that [are expanded to] include an interest rate' (p. 133–5). Similarly, VAR modelling has been criticized for the sensitivity of its predictive perform-ance to the choice of lag length.[34] Such sensitivity of results gives rise to great scepticism about the value of VAR modelling, even in its limited role as a forecasting tool.

Thirdly, Sims's preference for models which are triangularized but symmetric (in the sense of having the same lagged variables in each equation of the system) has been criticized on the grounds that it replaces one implausible restriction with another. For example, Cooley and LeRoy (1985) argue that 'explicit justification is necessary for whatever triangu-larity or orthogonality assumption is made – these are not arbitrary normalizations, but substantive restrictions on the parameter space that must be justified from theory' (p. 305). On a related point, Sachs (1982) critically observes that Sims's approach makes the 'astounding assump-tion' that the error terms are uncorrelated and that his specification allows 'all variables *in* the model ... to affect ... [each other (at least from lag one) whereas] all variables *outside* the model are captured by the error term and are allowed to affect [variables within the model] only in an arbitrary specified way' (p. 159), which depends on the triangularization.[35] Epstein (1987) goes further, claiming that the elements of the orthogonalized residuals, while mathematically correct, have no economic interpretation. 'They are analogous to variables in an ordinary regression constructed as principal components' (p. 215).

As Pagan (1987) is careful to point out, there are two separate issues here: one is the difficulty of giving any economic meaning to the orthogo-nal innovations and the other is the use of the orthogonalized innovations in the application of the VAR model. It has already been stated that one purpose of the models is to facilitate policy analysis and in this context, policy is interpreted very narrowly to mean the addition of a known innovation shock. The effects of different policies are isolated by rearrang-ing the system as a lower triangular Wold form.[36] However, there are problems of interpretation: on the one hand, VAR models are *presented* as having no reference to structural equations at all; on the other, VAR models *might* be considered as a reduced form system derived from structural equations. These two views are distinguished by Cooley and LeRoy (1985) as, respectively, non-structural models and structural models. They go on to argue that when 'the models are interpreted as structural, ... the restrictions on error distributions ... are not arbitrary renormalisations, but prior identifying restrictions. As such, they require justification from theory. Failing such justification (and it is seldom offered) the conclusions are equally without support' (p. 307).

If the models are interpreted as non-structural, the VAR itself becomes the structure and is no more than a superficially sophisticated summary of the historical correlations of the economic time series. As such, and assuming that the future is like the past, the representation may be useful for forecasting.[37] However, a characteristic of policy analysis is that the future may be unlike the past and the policy simulation is intended to track that difference.[38] As Sachs (1982, p. 158) notes 'In that case we need to know whether the historical correlations will hold up with policy changes.' If the correlations are invariant to the policy changes under consideration, then the effects of policy instruments cannot be quantified without imposing meaningful economic assumptions to identify relevant parameters. In essence, the policy conclusions are unsupportable because they are structural in nature and the VAR was intended to avoid the need for such assumptions about structure. VAR modelling is founded on a principle that since there is little reason to expect a shift in structure, one may as well use a VAR for forecasting since it parsimoniously describes the relevant historical experience.[39]

What has not been drawn out in these critiques is the fact that VAR has no role whatsoever in the hypothetico-deductive method of economic science; it can contribute few insights, if any, to our understanding of economic phenomena. Moreover VAR appears to be an example of extreme inductivism and is, therefore, wholly open to the charge of the inductivist critique: 'If a VAR predicts well, we do not know why it does so, nor what circumstances would, in the future, cause it to fail'. As a forecasting tool, it has used no explicit theory and no explicit assumptions, thus making it an example of measurement without theory or what Blaug has termed 'mindless instrumentalism': 'prediction is not necessarily explanation written forwards. Empirical work that fails utterly to discriminate between competing explanations quickly degenerates into a sort of mindless instrumentalism and it is not too much to say that the bulk of empirical work in modern economics is guilty on that score' (Blaug, 1980, p. 257).[40]

CAUSALITY

On the issue of causality testing, the focus of criticism is on Sims's use of Granger non-causality as equivalent to econometric exogeneity. But before discussing this, the more substantive point made by Cooley and

LeRoy should be made. Cooley and LeRoy distinguish between structural and non-structural models.[41] The point has already been made that the symmetric lag and triangularized specification are substantive restrictions if the VAR models are treated as structural systems. However, if the models are interpreted as non-structural, then these transformations are in fact arbitrary normalizations and, Sims would argue, do not require theoretical justification. This is a highly questionable methodological stance. Importantly then, Cooley and LeRoy argue that the model cannot be interpreted as doing more than summarizing the correlations in the data. Moreover, they conclude that 'no statement dealing with causation or the effect of interventions is admissible' (p. 306).

The argument that Granger non-causality is not sufficient for exogeneity has been made by several authors (see, for example Engle *et al.*, 1983; Leamer, 1985b; and Cooley and LeRoy, 1985).[42] Consider the relevant definitions: Sims's (1972) development of Granger's (1969) work on causality provides a relatively simple concept of non-causality; X Granger causes Y if, in a regression of Y on past, present and future values of X, all coefficients on future X values are insignificantly different from zero. Testing for causality/non-causality requires running the twin regressions of Y on past, present and future values of X; and of X on past, present and future values of Y. According to Sims, if X fails to Granger-cause Y then Y is exogenous to X. If additionally, Y Granger-causes X, then Y is considered causally prior to X. In this way Sims uses Granger non-causality as equivalent to econometric exogeneity. More formally, Cooley and LeRoy (1985) show that Granger non-causality is neither necessary nor sufficient for predeterminedness and it is necessary but not sufficient for strict exogeneity.[43]

Cooley and LeRoy (1985, pp. 289 and especially 296) argue that predeterminedness is the relevant exogeneity concept for the analysis of interventions.[44] Consider the structural VAR model:

$$x_t = a_1 y_t + a_2 x_{t-1} + a_3 y_{t-1} + u_{1t}$$
$$y_t = b_1 x_t + b_2 x_{t-1} + b_3 y_{t-1} + u_{2t}$$

if x is a predetermined variable ($a_1 = 0$) then an intervention consisting of varying x_t is unambiguously associated with a change in u_{1t}, and in no other exogenous variables. There is no necessity for x to be strictly exogenous ($a_1 = a_3 = 0$) to carry out the analysis: the effect on y_t is $b_1 \Delta x_t$ in both cases. More than this Cooley and LeRoy stress that '[g]iven predeterminedness, ... strict exogeneity ... is equivalent to Granger non-causality ... But for predeterminedness ... which is needed to justify any of the interventions under discussion, Granger non-causality is irrelevant...' (p. 298). Importantly then Cooley and LeRoy deny the validity of interpreting impulse response functions as reflecting causal orderings – the routine VAR method. Such interpretations would only be valid under assumptions of predeterminedness, for which theory has been employed. The claim that VAR methods are atheoretlcal cannot then be sustained.

If it is conceded that these problems with causality tests make them an unsatisfactory device for ordering variables in step IV of the approach, the only other option available to VAR practitioners is to fall back on *a priori* theory as in Sims (1980a, 1980b). However, this introduces a certain amount of logical inconsistency as much of 'the appeal of VAR models – *particularly to those more interested in econometrics than economics* – is that they appear to offer a way to generate the same kind of output as structural models, but without the input of explicit economic theory. This combination is indeed attractive, but if our analysis is correct it must be rejected as illusory' (Cooley and LeRoy, 1985, p. 306, emphasis added).[45]

Perhaps it should be stressed that these criticisms of the VAR approach do not deny it any uncontroversial applications. There certainly exist important applications of VAR models that generate conclusions which are invariant across observationally equivalent versions of the same model. For example, forecasts which are constructed directly from the reduced form will be invariant across observationally equivalent versions of a given model, although the competing models have *not* been tested one against another. Again VAR models can be used to determine the existence of Granger-causal orderings even in the absence of any theoretical reason to expect them; after all, Granger's (1969) test for causality is actually a two-variable VAR. The outcomes of such exercises can be viewed as stylized facts requiring subsequent explanation in terms of structural models and are therefore a method of 'hypothesis seeking'.[46] Of course, in one sense there is nothing new here; the traditional method tells us that econometric forecasts can be constructed from reduced forms and the exercise of hypothesis seeking is an old habit.

SOME METHODOLOGICAL OBSERVATIONS

Nevertheless, there are fundamental methodological objections to VAR modelling: no theory, beyond the definition of variables, is utilized in the approach and an immediate consequence of this is that no behavioural economic theories are stated in falsifiable form – therefore the approach is not a part of science. Moreover, any particular VAR representation is merely an inductively based conclusion and is open therefore to all the standard charges of inductivism. At one level, however, if a vector autoregression is interpreted as a reduced form of a structural model (as Cooley and LeRoy indicate it might), because the structure has never been established (and there are therefore no theoretical restrictions on the reduced form), there is no unique structure associated with any VAR. Indeed it may be the case that many structural forms, each representing a competing economic theory, are consistent with the VAR. In this sense the inductively based VAR is an exercise in confirmation; but because the users of VAR have never identified those conditions which could constitute a refutation of any structural form, the contribution of VAR to distinguishing between theories is nil.[47]

It might appear, however, that appeal to Granger/Sims causality has meaningful content. This can only be the case in the sense that there may be some empirical regularities (economic phenomena) deserving of further study, but VAR itself contributes nothing with regard to the scientific method of economics nor, surprisingly, do its proponents pretend anything different.

NOTES

1. See for example Brunner (1972), a volume based on two conferences held to examine the then current state of applied econometrics. Some of the key papers of the conference were very critical. In addition see Christ (1975) whose assessment of eleven models of the US economy led him to say '[the models] disagree so strongly about the effects of important monetary and fiscal policies that they cannot be considered reliable guides to such policy effects' (p. 54). However, see McNees (1982) for a rather different assessment: he writes 'the pendulum has now swung too far. The major models have been characterized as "meaningless", "without content", and providing "*no* useful information" about the economy. For these allegations to have content, there would have to be some superior, alternative models . . . the superiority of available, alternative techniques is yet to be demonstrated' (p. 47).
2. See for example, Cooper (1972) and Nelson (1972), both of whom demonstrate the good forecasting performance of univariate Box–Jenkins models relative to that of large econometric models.
3. 'At a practical level the Cowles Commission approach to the identification and estimation of simultaneous macroeconometric models has been questioned by Lucas and Sargent and by Sims, although from different viewpoints. . . . The response of the econometrics profession as a whole to the recent criticism has been to emphasize the development of more appropriate techniques, to use new data sets and to call for a better quality control of econometric research with special emphasis on model validation and diagnostic testing' (Pesaran, 1987b, p. 14). The reference to Lucas and

Sargent is to their work on the need to develop models consistent with rational expectations (Lucas, 1972, 1973; Sargent, 1973; see Pesaran, 1987a for a detailed discussion of the problems of identification and estimation of linear rational expectations models); the reference to Sims is Sims (1980) which is discussed in the text.

4. For examples of this early work, see the Koopmans and Hood volume (1953), particularly Marshak (1953) and Simon (1953). The task of establishing the identifiability of a system (however complex) rests on the ability to discover whether the system contains the appropriate number of restrictions. Typically the identification problem is assessed by using the rank and order conditions: the latter requires little more than counting included and excluded variables in each (structural) equation, but is in fact only a necessary condition. There are other means of identifying equations: for example, Maddala (1977) pp. 226–8 and Johnston (1972) pp. 365–72 discuss the use of restrictions on the contemporaneous variance–covariance matrix of the simultaneous equations system. Christ (1966) pp.334–43 discusses the use of restrictions on the range of an error term, knowledge of the ratio of two error term variances and knowledge of the covariance between two equations' error terms. Maddala (1977) pp. 228–31 discusses non-homogeneous restrictions, non-linearities and cross-equation restrictions. However, the relative ease of identification through zero restrictions has made it a most popular route.

5. This is not new to Sims, but a resurrection of arguments which can be found in Liu (1960).

6. Epstein (1987) provides a stimulating history of the formulation of structural models of the economy as systems of simultaneous equations, providing particular insights into the work carried out at the Cowles Commission in the 1940s and 1950s. Chapter 7 of Epstein's book is devoted to Sims's critique of structural estimation.

7. Epstein (1987) p. 61. Mann and Wald (1943) undertook to solve the problem of estimation of stationary linear stochastic difference equations in the most general terms. Haavelmo (1944) stressed the need for sufficient identifying information to enable successful estimation.

8. The precise route by which the final specification was determined is of great methodological interest but we are not currently in a position to report on this issue.

9. Notice that this is in direct opposition to the view presented in Chapter 4 of this book.

10. See Epstein (1987) p. 173. More recent analysis of exogeneity has made it clear that Koopman's conditions are sufficient but not necessary for consistent or efficient estimation of the equations for the endogenous variables; see Hatanaka and Odaki (1983), Engle, Hendry and Richard (1983) and the discussion of concepts of weak and strong exogeneity in Epstein *op. cit.*, pp. 174–5.

11. In the Cowles Commission approach exogeneity was assumed to be the property of the structural model, obtained from *a priori* theory. It was therefore not possible to test the identifying restrictions for they had to be assumed *a priori* and accepted on the basis of knowledge extraneous to the model under consideration (or as a matter of faith).

12. Fair (1987, p. 269). The first forecast was for year 1953.

13. The updating needs would be on a monthly or quarterly basis.

14. See for example Lucas (1972, 1973), Sargent (1973). Importantly the models could not be used to predict the impact of policy regime shifts and the focus of these writers was precisely this. Also note the point made by Pagan (1987) that the Cowles Commission researchers were themselves not unaware of the 'Lucas critique'; he refers the reader to Marschak (1953) and remarks that the limits of modelling 'somehow . . . got lost in the euphoria of the 1960s' (p. 20).

15. Lucas (1976).

16. See for example, Wallis (1980), Wickens (1982) and Pesaran (1987a).

17. 'In the presence of expectations, it turns out that the crutch of *a priori* knowledge of

lag lengths is indispensable, even when we have distinct strictly exogenous variables . . .' (Sims, 1980a, p. 7).

18. Sims (1980a) p. 11.
19. See Fisher (1961) pp. 140–1 for a neat presentation of this argument, which may be summarized as:

    (i) exclusion restrictions typically used for identification will 'at best, . . . only hold approximately, and approximately is not good enough' (p. 140). The equations are under-identified.

    (ii) few variables are truly exogenous, hence endogenous variables are being treated as if they were exogenous, hence the equations are really underidentified.

20. The restrictions could take several forms: they could view some components of y_t as exogenous and/or they could set some elements of the structural form matrices to zero.
21. As Epstein has noted, 'In this respect, the state of economic knowledge has not greatly improved since 1943 when Marschak admitted that no single theory deserved special credence' (Epstein, 1987, p. 207).
22. See Sargent (1979a) and Sargent (1979b, ch.XI) for an introduction to vector autoregressions.
23. Sometimes cross-equation restrictions are placed on the coefficients – but the restrictions are in general less restrictive than the exclusionary ones used by the traditional approach. This is discussed later in the text.
24. Webb (1984) compares forecasts from a simple VAR model with those from a consulting firm that uses a conventional model and with a series of consensus forecasts: the results were not conclusive but the editor of the special issue of *Economic Review* in which this study appeared was prepared to comment that 'the VAR model holds its own in the competition' (p.2).
25. See Bessler (1984) for a discussion of the lag selection problem.
26. By assertion, it cannot mean policy instruments in any other sense. Thus, the only effect of policy in a 'well specified' VAR is non-systematic.
27. In addition, no distinction is made between a shock of the classical statistical type, composed of innumerable small perturbing effects, and one that is a large change in a single variable that is not otherwise modelled.
28. Importantly, this is incompatible with the concept of *random* shocks! A shock is either random or engineered.
29. The concept of causality used here is not 'lay causality' but a technical definition adopted from Granger (1969).
30. See Leamer (1985b) for an interesting interpretation of Sims's ordering: 'Clearly, some economics is required to place any meaning on these variance decompositions. Parenthetically, I ask if Sims' (1980a) recursive ordering makes sense: money to real GNP, to unemployment, to wages, to prices, to import prices. It seems to me that he has in mind a rather traditional macro model, with IS-LM followed by Okun's Law followed by the Phillips curve followed by a price mark-up equation, with import prices thrown in as an afterthought' (p. 295).
31. As the variables on the right-hand side of each equation are predetermined, provided there are no constraints on the coefficients, OLS is an efficient estimation procedure and can be used on each equation.
32. Other uses of the VAR approach are: Bessler (1984); Bessler and Kling (1986); Chawdhury (1986); Litterman (1984,1986); Lupoletti and Webb (1986); Todd (1984); Webb (1984).
33. The usefulness of this technical concept of causality – Granger causality – is discussed later in the text.
34. See Doan *et al.*(1984), footnote 3 for some evidence.
35. Hendry (1985) makes the same point claiming that Sims's unrestricted equations 'mix

features which are relatively variable with those which are potentially more constant, rendering the whole non-constant' (p. 73). Thus it is unlikely that one could develop VAR models which are stable, in the sense of being constant representations of the data over time.

36. Goldfeld (1982) develops this point as follows: 'One difficulty is that these estimates are not invariant to the ordering of the equations in the VAR model. This is a troublesome feature of the VAR approach, and it would be nice to know the sensitivity of the estimates to the causal ordering' (p. 156).

37. See the discussion of induction in Chapter 2 of this book.

38. This is reiteration of the standard Hume critique (see the references noted in Chapter 2, note 7).

39. See Sachs (1982) pp. 158–9 for a neat example. In defence, Sims (1986) concedes that 'it is impossible to use a statistical model to analyze policy without going behind the correlations to make an economic interpretation of them' (p. 3) but argues that 'there is a trade-off between types of models for policy analysis, not a hierarchy of them' (p. 15).

40. Blaug goes on: 'A wild exaggeration? Perhaps, but there are many others who have said as much. Kenen (1975, p. xvi) expresses the same thought in forceful language:

> I detect a dangerous ambiguity in our quantitative work. We do not distinguish carefully enough between the *testing* of hypotheses and the estimation of structural relationships. The ambiguity is rampant in economics. . . . We should be spending more time and thought on the construction of tests that will help us to discriminate between hypotheses having different economic implications. It is not enough to show that our favourite theory does as well as – or better than – some other theory when it comes to accounting retrospectively for the available evidence' (Blaug, 1980, p. 257).

Note the similarities here with the arguments presented in Chapter 5 on Hendry's work.

41. 'Our complaint about atheoretical macroeconometrics can now be summarised. It is that the distinction between structural and non-structural models is not observed' (Cooley and LeRoy, 1985, pp. 305–6).

42. The inadequacy of Granger causality from the point of view of the more philosophical notions of causation are discussed by Zellner (1979).

43. Even if one were to ignore the incorrectness of inferring exogeneity from causality tests problems still exist with the causality tests themselves. See Feige and Pearce (1979), Geweke *et al.* (1983) and Thornton and Batten (1985).

44. Where interventions are distinct from innovations.

45. It should be noted that in Sims (1982) the premise of structural stability in the VAR approach was abandoned: the coefficients of the model are assumed to follow independent random walks. The action is defended in Doan *et al.* (1984), but note Epstein's view: 'It is a remarkable substitution of statistics for economic theory as an explanation of economic change' (Epstein, 1987, p. 219).

46. Eichenbaum (1985) argues that unconstrained vector autoregressions may serve as a motivation for the construction of theoretical models: for example, he views McCallum's (1983) interpretation of Sims's results regarding the role of money on economic activity as just such an example.

47. 'The great difficulty with the VAR is that it does not appear to provide an effective means for reducing the level of economic ignorance. Rather than resolving different theories of macroeconomic structure, it essentially ignores them and retreats to economic hypotheses that are so broad and known to be incomplete that they virtually defy critical test' (Epstein, 1987, p. 219).

8. Cointegration

Writing in 1987, Pesaran observed that:

> Since the early applications of the correlation analysis to economics data by Yule and Hooker, the serial dependence of economic time series and the problem of spurious correlation that it gave rise to had been the single most important factor explaining the profession's scepticism concerning the value of regression analysis in economics (1987b, p.12).

It is not therefore surprising that research in the analysis of economic time-series data has sought 'solutions' to the spurious correlation problem. In the post-war years this programme involved both the development of particular econometric techniques, for example the well known Cochrane – Orcutt method for the computation of regression coefficients under the assumption that the errors followed a first order autoregressive process, and the development of tests for serial correlation.[1] More recent work has developed into time-series modelling, for example, the development of Box–Jenkins techniques although practitioners of time-series modelling explicitly acknowledge its distant relationship with econometric modelling. For example, Harvey writes:

> There are two aspects to the study of time series – analysis and modelling. The aim of analysis is to summarise the properties of a series and to characterise its salient features. ... The distinguishing feature of a time series model, as opposed, say, to an econometric model, is that no attempt is made to relate y_t to other variables. The movements in y_t are 'explained' solely in terms of its own past, or by its position in relation to time (Harvey, 1981, p.l).

Cointegration has evolved from the long-recognized knowledge that with stochastic trends in the variables, the usual techniques of regression analysis can result in misleading inferential conclusions.[2] One claimed benefit of using cointegration techniques is the ability to employ rules of thumb to evaluate the results of regression analysis using variables which have stochastic trends. Other perceived roles for cointegration techniques derive from the view that much economic theory can be characterized as a study of long-run relationships[3] and that the statistical notion of 'cointegration' of time series corresponds to the theoretical notion of a long-run equilibrium relationship. These claims are discussed more fully below but, first, some terms should be explained.

FROM STOCHASTIC TRENDS TO COINTEGRATED VARIABLES

A variable which is increasing by a fixed amount (say 3 per cent per time period) on average but has an unpredictable random component is said to have a stochastic trend. Equivalently, the variable could be described as following a random walk with drift. Denoting the variable at time t by x_t, suppose:

$$x_t = \mu + x_{t-1} + e_t$$

where e_t is serially uncorrelated, with constant, finite variance, μ is the average, predictable drift. Therefore, if x_t represents the log of GNP, then the average predictable growth of GNP, $(x_t - x_{t-1})$, is μ but there is an unpredictable random component represented by e_t.

In the above example, the variable x has a distribution which depends on time and is therefore defined to be non-stationary. When the non-stationary variable x_t can be written:

$$x_t = \mu + x_{t-1} + u_t$$

where u_t is stationary (but not necessarily serially uncorrelated), then the variable is said to be integrated of order one I (1). This is because any non-stationary variable whose first difference $(x_t - x_{t-1})$ is stationary is said to be integrated of order one. It should be noted that all variables which have a stochastic trend are integrated variables.[4] One important feature of an integrated process is that its variance tends to infinity as t increases.[5]

The concept of cointegration (due to Granger, 1981) derives from a consideration of the statistical properties of some linear combination of two integrated variables: if there is some linear combination (weighted average) of two integrated variables which is stationary, then the two time series are said to be cointegrated. Thus, if the two variables x_t and y_t each contain a stochastic trend, they can each be described as integrated variables; if further, the variable $(x_t - \alpha y_t)$ is stationary, the two variables are described as cointegrated.

The prescriptive message from the proponents of cointegration techniques in applied econometric practice is to establish the integration properties of time-series variables at the outset of an empirical investigation. In practice there is already some evidence which suggests that many macroeconomic variables, when viewed as univariate time series, appear to be integrated, for example Nelson and Plosser (1982) find evidence to support the view that many macroeconomic variables appear to be I(l). Additionally, to the extent that ARIMA$(p,1,q)$ models seem to characterize many macroeconomic variables, and because Box–Jenkins ARIMA$(p,1,q)$ models are 1st-order integrated variables (with order p autoregressive and order q moving average components), it follows that the growth in these variables can be described by stochastic trends.[6] Such variables may therefore be written as the sum of a random walk (with drift) and a stationary time series, e.g:

$$y_t = y^p_t + y^s_t$$
where y^p_t is a random walk (with drift) and
y^s_t is a stationary series.

THE NATURE OF INFERENTIAL PROBLEMS

The usual assumptions of time-series analysis are that (i) the error term is serially uncorrelated and is uncorrelated with the regressors; and that (ii) all the regressors are either deterministic or stationary random variables. On the basis of these assumptions, the estimated coefficients will be consistent and, in large samples, the null distribution of regression t and F statistics can be approximated by normal and F distributions respectively. If either (i) or (ii) are false assumptions, these results do not hold: (i) is testable (see, for example, Pesaran and Pesaran, 1987); yet (ii) is more a matter of judgement. Consider the observation that a variable x_t grows through time; this observation is an empirically derived, inferential statement and, as such, it requires explanation. There is a matter of judgement involved in labelling x_t as a variable which has a stochastic trend: it may be that more exhaustive analysis would reveal determinants of x_t that would render x_t to be a 'non-stochastic' process. Similarly, there is a judgement involved if x_t is viewed as an integrated process for it may be that further exhaustive analysis of x_t may 'discover' its determinants as a 'non-stochastic' process. Chapter 1 has discussed the notion of random variables as a method by which to model ignorance; if this is accepted, then integrated variables reflect a very high, and unacceptably high, level of ignorance, as do all time-series models. Nevertheless, Stock and Watson (1988) refer to variables which have stochastic trends (are integrated processes), and consider their use in regression analysis. They note that assumptions (i) and (ii) may be violated, and go on to explain that if one knows which variables have stochastic trends, which do not, and whether the trends are common, then there are some results which can be employed to evaluate regression results (with integrated variables). Their application is, however, not uncontentious; the results are:

1.   When some or all of the regressors are integrated processes, condition (ii) does not apply. However, the OLS estimator will be consistent and the standard critical values from the t and F distributions apply to the coefficients of interest provided that either the coefficients of interest are coefficients on mean zero stationary variables or the coefficients of interest can become coefficients on mean zero stationary variables through rewriting the regression equation.

2.   When the parameter of interest is a coefficient on an integrated process and cannot be written as a stationary variable, the estimator of the coefficient of interest is consistent, but the usual critical values do not apply.

3.   When the integrated dependent variable is cointegrated with at least one of the integrated regressors, condition (i) may not hold because the error in the regression, whilst stationary, is not necessarily serially uncorrelated nor independent of the regressors.

4.   When the integrated dependent variable is cointegrated with at least one of the integrated regressors and the coefficients of interest are, or can be expressed as, coefficients on mean zero stationary variables, then (unless the regressor is strictly exogenous) the stationary regressor will typically be correlated with the error term and the parameter estimate will be inconsistent.[7] Most importantly, however, when the parameter of interest is a coefficient on an integrated process and cannot be written as a coefficient on a stationary variable, then the estimator of the coefficient of interest is consistent although the asymptotic theory is not standard.[8] This result is fundamental to the 'cointegration' procedure, for it specifies that when the dependent variable and a regressor are each integrated processes *and are cointegrated* then the ordinary least squares regression estimator is consistent.

5.   When the dependent variable and at least one regressor are inte-

grated, but there is no cointegrating relationship, the error term in the regression is integrated. If the parameter of interest is a coefficient on an integrated process which cannot be written as a coefficient on a stationary variable then these coefficients will not be consistent but will converge to random variables. This result, too, is crucial to the cointegration procedure, for it provides a test of cointegration: if in a regression of two integrated variables, the error term is itself integrated then *there is no cointegrating relationship between the variables of interest, and the parameter estimator is not consistent, but converges to a random variable.*

The perceived benefits of pre-testing for integrated and cointegrated processes derive from the results listed above. Arguably, this should facilitate the interpretation of OLS regressions run on time-series data.[9]

COINTEGRATION AND LONG-RUN EQUILIBRIUM

The cointegration properties of time-series variables are also thought to provide a procedure for testing some economic hypotheses and facilitating empirical investigation at the model specification stage. These potential uses derive from the view that economic theory proposes forces (such as market forces) which imply that some combinations of time series will not diverge from each other by too great an extent, at least in the long-run.

> Examples of such variables are interest rates on assets of different maturities, prices of a commodity in different parts of the country, income and expenditure by local government and the value of sales and production costs of an industry. Other possible examples would be prices and wages, imports and exports, market prices of substitute commodities, money supply and prices and spot and future prices of a commodity. ... in each case the correctness of the beliefs about long-term relatedness is an empirical question (Granger, 1986, p. 213).

Exploiting the view that the statistical notion of 'cointegration' of time series corresponds to the theoretical notion of a long-run equilibrium relationship arguably gives rise to a means by which certain propositions from economic theory can be tested. Consider two series x_t and y_t each of which are integrated of order one, I(1), and therefore each has infinite variance. If economic theory suggests a long-run equilibrium relationship:

$$y_t - \alpha x_t = 0,$$

then a linear combination of the two series is stationary. Moreover, not only are the two series cointegrated but their cointegration 'is at least a *necessary* condition for them to have a stable long-run linear relationship' for otherwise x_t and y_t will tend to drift apart without bound (Taylor, 1988, p.1373, emphasis added). It is important to examine this statement; it suggests that the existence of a stable long-run relationship between two integrated variables implies that they are also cointegrated.

Consider the following:

$$y_t = \alpha x_t + \beta Z_t + \text{error}$$

where, in the sample, $t = 1 \ldots T$, the values of Z_t and the error are both stationary. If analysis is confined to this period then the stable relationship between y_t and x_t implies cointegration between these variables. Outside this sample, nothing guarantees that Z will remain stationary: were estimation to use a sample larger than a sample $(1, \ldots, T)$, then, although the long-run stable relationship between y_t and x_t is unaltered, examining them only as a pair will not result in the observation of 'cointegration' if, for $t > T$, Z_t is not stationary. To what does the adjective 'stable' refer? Is it the 'relationship' or the 'long-run'? In our example, the relationship is stable, but the 'environment' is not; thus, in this simple presentation, the conditions which ensure that the 'long-run environment' is itself stable are violated since the behaviour of the variable Z is not stable. Thus, stability of a long-run relationship (by which is meant *both* the stability of the relationship *and* the stability of the long-run conditions) may be seen to imply cointegration. However, this concept of the long run has no material, protocol, counterpart for we are never in a position to suggest that the long run is stable. This last remark takes its truth from the standard inductivist critique: even if it has been observed that the 'environment' is stable in a particular sample, to conclude that the 'long run' is then stable would be fallacious.

The proposition that cointegration is at least necessary for the existence of a stable long-run relationship is, therefore, only true within a very narrow definition which restricts the nature of the 'long run'. Effectively, the error term in the cointegrating equation is capturing the effects of all influences not otherwise modelled explicitly; the error term is, therefore, picking up *inter alia* the consequences of the failure of the 'real world' to conform to the world of *ceteris paribus*. Because the method of cointegration relegates some systematic influences to the error term (the only requirement of the error is that it be stationary, rather than non–systematic), the inductively based 'knowledge' drawn from the cointegrating equation is inadequate. It is inadequate because it utilizes a concept of the long run which has no material counterpart, but, more importantly, were a cointegrating relationship found, the investigator has an insufficient understanding of why that relationship 'works' and, consequently, has no understanding of the conditions which would cause that relationship to break down. Moreover, the method falls to identify those events which would 'falsify' the hypothesized relationship: *if cointegration is not observed this may be because the auxiliary hypotheses have been inadequately treated leading to a non-systematic and non-stationary error term even in the presence of a stable relationship between the variables of interest.* Thus, the lack of cointegration is insufficient evidence on which to refute the hypothesized relationship.

As an example of the cointegration approach in practice, consider Taylor (1988) who uses cointegration techniques to test the purchasing power parity hypothesis as a long-run equilibrium condition. He correspondingly tests for stationarity of the process

$$g_t = e_t - \alpha p_t$$

where e_t is the logarithm of the nominal exchange rate (domestic price of foreign exchange) at time t,

p_t is the ratio of the domestic to the foreign price level and where α is allowed to deviate from unity because the long-run proportionality between the exchange rate and relative prices may not be strictly one-to-one as a result of measurement error and transportation costs. If g_t is a zero-mean, stationary process, then in long-run equilibrium the nominal exchange rate will be proportional to relative prices, but a 1 per cent increase in the relative price ratio will lead to an α per cent long-run depreciation of the exchange rate.[10]

The testing is a step-wise procedure: the first task is to test the two hypotheses that e_t is integrated of order one and p_t is integrated of order one. This is done by running the two regressions:

$$\Delta e_t = \beta_1 e_{t-1} + \sum_{j=1}^{m} \gamma_{1j} \Delta e_{t-j} + u_{1t}$$

$$\Delta p_t = \beta_2 p_{t-1} + \sum_{j=1}^{m} \gamma_{2j} \Delta p_{t-j} + u_{2t}$$

where, in each case, m is selected to be large enough to ensure that the residuals are each empirical white noise. The test statistic is the ratio of $\hat{\beta}$

to its calculated standard error obtained from an OLS regression. In essence, the decision rule is to reject the null hypothesis if β_i is significantly negative.[11]

The next step[12] is to run the 'cointegration regression':

$$e_t = \alpha + \beta p_t + u_t$$

and test the null hypothesis that the residuals are integrated of order one.[13] On the basis of the above procedure Taylor concluded 'we fail to find cointegration between the nominal exchange rate and relative prices for any of the countries examined ... we obtained results extremely unfavourable to the PPP hypothesis' (pp. 1376–7). This inference is interesting from a methodological perspective for it is a clear demonstration of the limitations of using cointegration techniques for hypothesis testing. The time-series analysis (cointegration), of itself, cannot be used for testing economic hypotheses as it fails to *model* the auxiliary hypotheses. The comments above identify why a lack of cointegration cannot be used to falsify hypotheses; particularly, in this example, it is important to note that Taylor chose to model the role of transportation costs by allowing α to differ from unity, therefore presuming that transportation costs can be modelled as if they are constant; yet it is possible to take the view that these transport costs are *not* constant (in which case their impact would have been modelled by the introduction of an additional variable). Taylor's presumption is an auxiliary hypothesis in disguise which should be tested: if his presumption should be rejected in favour of the alternative presented here, then the variability of transport costs is being picked up in the error term which is used in the cointegration test. It is therefore possible that the result of the 'cointegration test' would have been different had he made a different auxiliary hypothesis. What is important here is to recognize that because cointegration fails to model auxiliary hypotheses it *cannot* lead to any firm conclusions.[14] The inference made by Taylor is only valid in the context of a very narrow vision, and that vision is itself testable in principle.

Engle and Granger (1987) provide several empirical examples, one of which is claimed to be a test of the quantity theory, $MV = PY$, carried out by testing the hypothesis: nominal money and nominal GNP are cointegrated, against the alternative hypothesis that the two variables are not cointegrated. Their argument takes the following form: 'Empirical implications stem from the assumption that velocity is constant or at least stationary. Under this condition, log M, log P and log Y should be cointegrated with known unit parameters. Similarly, nominal money and nominal GNP should be co-integrated' (p.274).[15] The points made above about the auxiliary hypotheses being hidden in the cointegration approach are again pertinent here.

The above examples focused on just one way in which the cointegration properties of time-series variables have been utilized: another use may be as part of an econometric modelling exercise. For example Engle and Granger (1987) state that 'it may be sensible to test [whether a set of variables are cointegrated] ... before estimating a multivariate dynamic model' (p.264). Again, Granger (1986) states that 'A test for cointegration can be thought of as a pre-test to avoid "spurious regression" situations' (p.226). Utilizing cointegration properties as part of an econometric modelling exercise is an attempt to exploit the link between cointegration and long-run equilibrium[16] when analysing integrated variables: consider the case where the two series x_t and y_t are both integrated of order one and which are cointegrated: there exists a linear combination, $z_t = (y_t - Ax_t)$, which is stationary. Because the long-run, 'equilibrium', relationship suggested by economic theory can be presented as $y_t = Ax_t$ then z_t measures the extent to which the system (x_t, y_t) is out of equilibrium and Granger (1986) terms this the 'equilibrium error'. Moreover, Hendry notes that, because A is unique, z_t 'seems a feasible way to retain "long-run" information in an I(O) representation' (Hendry,1986, p.202). The mechanism by which this is supposed to have an impact on model specification is through a type of dynamic model favoured by time-series econometricians, the so-called 'error correction' models. Engle and Granger (1987) prove that if two variables, say x_t, y_t are both I(l) and are cointegrated then there always exists a generating mechanism having the 'error correcting' form:

$$\Delta x_t = -\rho_1 Z_{t-1} + \text{lagged}\,(\Delta x_t,\, \Delta y_t) + d(B)\varepsilon_{1t}$$
$$\Delta y_t = -\rho_2 Z_{t-1} + \text{lagged}\,(\Delta x_t, \Delta y_t) + d(B)\varepsilon_{2t}$$

where $Z_t = x_t - Ay_t$.

Moreover, data presented in an error-correction model must be cointegrated. Granger (1986) notes that it is possible to exploit the 'equilibrium error' in model building allowing

the introduction of the impact of long-run or 'equilibrium' economic theories into the models used by the time-series analysts to explain[17] the short-run dynamics of economic data. The resulting error-correction models should produce better short-run forecasts and will certainly produce long-run forecasts that hold together in economically meaningful ways (Granger,1986, p.226).

The prescriptive message is therefore to test for cointegration of variables and use the information in the subsequent specification of the model.

CONCLUSION

Cointegration is wholly open to the charge of being 'measurement without theory': it is presented as if it will purge economic series of internal dependencies and that this is desirable; but these internal dependencies represent inductive knowledge. Take, for example, the first stage of testing cointegration - testing for unit roots: this is no more than seeking to find a relationship within a univariate time series. If it is found that x_t is related to x_{t-1} then, of itself, this contains no proposition about economics and certainly no explicit economic hypotheses have been erected to be knocked down. The advocates of cointegration seem to assume that univariate time series have their own data generating process which is independent of theoretical considerations; this view has been examined in Chapter 5 and has been criticized at length there. Suffice here to say that it is difficult to see how our understanding of economic behaviour can be deepened by concepts of time-series modelling; although it *does* prompt questions of interest, for example 'why is a variable capable of being modelled as I(1)?'.

Two 'cointegrated' variables move together and, *ceteris paribus*, they do not drift apart. Advocates of cointegration techniques effectively choose to model the 'failure' of the *ceteris paribus* clause by a stationary error term (rather than a non-systematic error term) and do not enquire further of the role of the error. However, as argued above, the systematic components of the error may, through the appropriate analysis of the (implicit) auxiliary hypotheses, lead to an understanding of the process, rather than lead simply to an inductively based conclusion.

From an economist's perspective, an important limitation of time-series analysis is that *there is no inquiry as to how integrated processes arise*. Indeed, no concepts of economics are utilized in the first stages of a cointegration study (that is, in the tests for univariate economic time series to be integrated) and, even in the later stages, economic theory is accepted throughout as a maintained hypothesis. It therefore seems that cointegration represents only 'inductive' information: the final equations can only be used to 'verify' economic theory because cointegration does not identify any conditions which would properly lead to a falsification. Moreover, we do not know why any particular cointegrating relationship 'works' (because the economic hypotheses appear only in disguise) and, therefore, we do not know what conditions in the future would cause it to fail.

In this sense, it should be recognized that practitioners are choosing to exploit the inductively inferred properties of univariate time series and that this runs counter to a methodologically sound procedure (which demands the specification of auxiliary hypotheses explicitly in order to test the main hypotheses). In the approach of the 'cointegrators' the auxiliary hypotheses are disguised, subsumed in the concept of 'integrated variables' and in stationary, non-white noise errors while the main hypothesis is translated into the concept of cointegration *per se*. The starting point of the approach fails to utilize the concepts and hypotheses of economic theory and the later stages do not offer a method of falsification. As such, this approach cannot be seen as a part of the hypothetico-deductive method and, therefore, is not capable of furthering our understanding of economic phenomena; therefore cointegration techniques can contribute nothing to the task of distinguishing between theories.

What the concepts of integration and cointegration do offer, however, is a challenge to economists to address questions such as 'If the variable y_t may be described by an integrated process of order 1, then what does this mean? What *economic* hypotheses (as opposed to mere statistical descriptions) explain this phenomenon?' Failure to recognize such questions results in measurement without theory and inductivism; importantly, economics, allied to econometric techniques, are capable of addressing these questions within a methodologically sound approach.

NOTES

1. See Cochrane and Orcutt (1949) and Durbin and Watson (1950, 1951). Much of this work was carried out at the Department of Applied Economics at Cambridge, UK under the direction of Richard Stone.
2. See Yule (1926) for a discussion of the time-series problems of spurious or hidden correlation; also Hendry (1986) for a statement of the historical development.
3. For a much fuller discussion of the study of long-run relationships, see Chapter 5 in this book.
4. A non-stationary variable which needs to be differenced d times to be stationary is said to be integrated of order d. A variable that is integrated is said to have a unit root in its autoregressive representation, which simply refers to the unit coefficient on x_{t-1} in the formula defining a simple integrated process. The terms 'x_t has one unit root' and 'x_t is integrated of order one' are wholly equivalent.
5. See Engle and Granger (1987) p.253.
6. Beveridge and Nelson (1981) prove that every variable having an ARIMA $(p, 1, q)$ representation contains a random walk stochastic trend.

7. This is the usual source of 'simultaneous equations bias', 'errors in variables bias' and 'omitted variables bias'.
8. See Fuller (1976) and Dickey and Fuller (1979) for a discussion.
9. See Stock and Watson (1988) for a demonstration of the use of this framework for explaining a set of regression results.
10. Taylor (1988) derives some motivation for allowing α to differ from unity by examining simple models of measurement error and/or transportation costs. He fully acknowledges that his analysis is highly stylized; what is not explicitly recognized is that he has actually made an important methodological presumption at this stage. See the discussion later in the text.
11. However, the test statistic does not have a t-distribution but tables of significance levels have been provided by Dickey and Fuller (1979). If one cannot reject the hypothesis that the (logarithms of the) nominal exchange rate and the ratio of price indices are I(1) series, then it is permissible to proceed to the test for cointegration.
12. There are other methods of testing for cointegration see Engle and Granger (1987) pp. 264–270. See Pesaran and Pesaran (1987) for a clear presentation of the procedures involved in testing for unit roots and cointegration (Lessons 24, 25: pp. 125–30)
13. Using either D–F statistics or augmented D–F statistics or the DW statistic.
14. These issues are discussed more fully in the concluding section of this chapter.
15. Engle and Granger (1987) summarize their results: 'In a series of examples it is found that consumption and income are co-integrated, wages and prices are not, short and long interest rates are, and nominal GNP is co-integrated with M2, but not M1, M3, or aggregate liquid assets' (p.251).
16. It is important to note the very particular way in which 'long-run equilibrium' is defined in this context.
17. In our view it is incorrect to use the word 'explain' here as the practice is actually one of 'inductively derived description'.

9. Summary

Econometrics is that branch of economics which explicitly unites deduction, induction and statistical inference; its methodology concerns the procedures adopted in the testing and, where applicable, the quantification of economic theories. The development of econometrics is largely a post-Second World War phenomenon, exploiting the increased availability of economic data, high speed computers and appropriate software. However, its development was structured by an increasing awareness amongst economists of the work in the philosophy of science, especially that of Sir Karl Popper. Indeed, the methodology of econometrics is, perhaps, best understood via the sophisticated falsificationism of Popper. Popper offered, *inter alia,* a demarcation criterion between science and non-science, designating science as that body of synthetic propositions regarding the real world which, at least in principle, are capable of refutation through the use of empirical observations.

During the 1960s especially, the methodology of economics appeared to be based upon a superficial appeal to Popperian falsificationism and some economists held the hope that econometrics would facilitate the establishment of an empirical base similar in content to that of the hard sciences. In econometrics many saw what they perceived as the provision of a rigorous and reliable method of testing hypotheses, a clear-cut route by which 'poor' theories would be weeded out to be replaced by better theories. This hope was firmly based upon a falsificationist methodology in which econometrics was to provide the evidence on which refutation would take place. In contrast many, if not the majority, of econometric investigations in the 1960s and 1970s were directed more towards the estimation of economic models than towards the testing of hypotheses. In practice, therefore, econometrics became a vehicle for verification, but used the rhetoric of falsification.

The framework developed for the testing of hypotheses in the natural sciences is essentially probabilistic and econometrics has adopted, and in part adapted, the methodology implicit in the non-determinist, statistical, model. However, that methodology typically utilizes a repeated sampling reference which can have no material counterpart in a non-experimental context. This has led some commentators to take a nihilistic stance towards

145

econometrics; however, that particular stance is rejected in this text. Chapter 1 argues that it is possible to use a subjective probability approach, as opposed to the 'objective probability' approach of the repeated sampling framework, in order to capture the 'degrees of belief' held by an investigator regarding those components of a model not otherwise explicitly modelled. Thus, in this approach, the 'error term' of a regression model is deemed to behave as if it were the result of drawing independent samples from a random variable (independent of the regressors) having a zero mean and constant variance. The 'population' in question is hypothetical. This judgement allows hypotheses of interest to be tested within the familiar statistical framework and, most importantly, it identifies as an appropriate model one within which those components not modelled explicitly may be viewed as independent drawings from a white noise stochastic variable. (This statement is made for the case of a single equation model: if the model is most appropriately examined as a simultaneous model then a number of the 'regressors' are also modelled and the 'error terms' are to be treated as if they were the result of drawing independent values from a constant variance, zero mean, random variable which is independent of the exogenous regressors.)

Chapter 2 proceeds to examine the limits and challenges to econometrics by exploring the nature of scientific explanation using first a deterministic framework and then a probabilistic framework. If an hypothesis is stated in deterministic form and tested within a deterministic model, then one refutation of the predictions of the hypothesis is sufficient evidence upon which to claim a refutation of that hypothesis. (It does not, however, follow that a confirming instance implies full acceptance of that hypothesis since there is no logic of confirmation.) Now hypotheses in economics are typically not stated in deterministic form, but as tendencies and are tested within a stochastic model.

This generates two particular complications: first, a probabilistic hypothesis rules out almost no observed events and second, the validity of any statistic is itself dependent upon the validity of a set of crucial assumptions. The former complication can only be dealt with by identifying those events which are, under the truth of the hypothesis, deemed highly improbable and thus deemed to be evidence against the hypothesis: this is the essence of 'practical falsification' by which, given the truth of the hypothesis, the adoption of a methodological norm effectively rules out some events. The latter complication comprises the phenomenon of 'pre-test bias' and this, too, can only be dealt with, given our current statistical technological apparatus, by the adoption of a methodological norm.

The issue has been more fully described earlier, but some reiteration is necessary: the validity of any statistic depends upon the validity of certain assumptions and those assumptions may, themselves, be tested. If those prior tests lead to a non-rejection of the required assumptions then the main hypothesis of interest may itself be tested; however, the tests of the assumptions are liable to error, and a non-rejection of a null hypothesis may be the subject of a Type II error – thus the ultimate test which is carried out has validity only when no Type II errors have been made at the pre-test stage. Ignoring the possibility of error at the pre-test stage gives rise to bias in the ultimate test, hence the label 'pre-test bias'. From a purely technical standpoint, there is no ready answer to this issue; however, it may be approached informally. There are two particular problems to be addressed: first, the pre-tests require the investigator to proceed on the basis of a confirmation of a null hypothesis, and we recognize that there is no logic of confirmation; second, the possibility of having committed an error at the pretest stage should be incorporated in the final test procedure. Regarding the first issue, progress can only be made by introducing a methodological norm of confirmation (analogous to the methodological norm required in moving from naive falsification to sophisticated practical falsification). On the second issue, progress can only be made by a tempering of one's conclusions: confident conclusions based upon the assertion that no Type II errors have been committed are wholly inappropriate and must be replaced by less confident statements which implicitly recognize the pretest nature of the process.

Thus the limits of econometrics are a consequence of the use of stochastic models, the consequent need for methodological norms by which to make operational the process of falsification, and the recognition of pre-test bias which itself requires the use of methodological norms of confirmation and demands that conclusions be phrased in non-dogmatic language which avoids the confidence of an earlier era. This view, then, treats currently maintained hypotheses as the basis of our knowledge but recognizes that what is currently maintained is the consequence of the use of specific methodological norms; therein lie the limits of econometrics. The challenge to econometrics lies in the recognition that we cannot be at all sure that those maintained hypotheses are the best which are available; one of the most important roles which econometricians can therefore fulfil lies in the search for, and identification of, better scientific theories of economic phenomena.

This is, of course, a rather different emphasis from that popularized in the 1960s by the 'positivists' and 'operationalists'; Chapter 3 focuses on the rise in the popularity of econometrics in the optimistic climate of 'positive economics'. The remainder of this book examines the various econometric practices which currently prevail: the 'traditional textbook' approach (Chapter 4), followed by chapters dealing with those practices championed by Hendry (Chapter 5), Leamer (Chapter 6), Sims (Chapter 7) and the 'cointegrators' (Chapter 8). With the exception of the traditional approach, each of these popular practices has specific methodological weaknesses when viewed in the context of the material presented in Chapters 1 and 2; this book advocates the traditional approach as the preferred econometric strategy. However, the typical presentation of the traditional approach has a number of critical weaknesses (which have, themselves, been significant in the development of the 'competing' strategies discussed in this book). The purpose of Chapter 4 was to recast the 'traditional' approach into a methodologically acceptable strategy and the modifications are summarized below.

With few modifications it is possible to restate 'traditional econometric modelling' within a falsificationist methodology; these modifications include *inter alia* the recognition of the role of auxiliary hypotheses in the testing of a main hypothesis and the recognition of the status of the 'error term' in a regression equation. One of the important points to be made regarding the role of auxiliary hypotheses is that any main hypothesis may be phrased within a large variety of regression equations, depending on the particular treatment of the auxiliary hypotheses. Regarding the error term, the approach adopted here has been to treat any regression equation as a decomposition of the determinants of the dependent variable into that due to a set of regressors (the systematic component) and an error term which is wholly non-systematic. Within this framework, therefore, it is necessary to confirm the correctness of the specification of a regression equation as a prerequisite to the testing of a main hypothesis of interest. Thus, in addition to the familiar issue of practical falsification, it is essential that the specification of the model in which the main hypothesis is tested has been confirmed as correct; 'practical falsification' therefore requires not only methodological norms which set the criteria of rejection, but also methodological norms which set the criteria of confirmation.

In the process of confirmation various statistical tests of the specification are made. If any test indicates a weakness of the specification then such test results only indicate the need for a re-specification; they do not indicate the direction of re-specification. In order to identify or determine appropriate directions of re-specification, the investigator must re-examine the treatment of the auxiliary hypotheses and re-cast the main hypothesis in a new model which treats the auxiliary hypotheses differently. Only when a model's specification has been 'confirmed' can the main hypothesis of interest be tested. As is fully described in Chapter 4, this demands both an iterative procedure and the use of methodological norms within the familiar framework of statistical testing.

References

Anderson, L.C. and Carlson, K. (1970) 'A monetarist model for economic stabilisation', Federal Reserve Bank of St Louis, *Review,* 52, 7–25.

Archibald, G.C. (1959) 'The state of economic science', *British Journal for Philosophy of Science,* 10, 58–69.

Archibald, G.C. (1960) 'Testing marginal productivity theory', *Review of Economic Studies,* 27, 210–13.

Archibald, G.C. (1961) 'Chamberlin versus Chicago', *Review of Economic Studies,* 29, 2–28.

Archibald, G.C. (1963) 'Reply to Chicago', *Review of Economic Studies,* 30, 68–71.

Archibald, G.C. (1966) 'Refutation or comparison?', *British Journal for Philosophy of Science,* 17, 279–96.

Ashenfelter, O. and Card, D. (1982) 'Time series representations of economic variables and alternative models of the labour market', *Review of Economic Studies,* 49, 761–82.

Bell, D. and Kristol, I. (1981) *The Crisis in Economic Theory,* New York: Basic Books.

Bessler, D.A. (1984) 'Relative prices and money: A vector autoregression on Brazilian data', *American Journal of Agricultural Economics,* 66, 25–30.

Besslers, D.A. and Kling, J.L. (1986) 'Forecasting vector autoregressions with Bayesian priors', *American Journal of Agricultural Economics,* 68, 144–51.

Beveridge, S. and Nelson, C.R. (1981) 'A new approach to decomposition of economic time series into permanent and transitory components with particular attention to measurement of the "Business Cycle"', *Journal of Monetary Economics,* 7, 151–74.

Blaug, M. (1980) *The Methodology of Economics. Or How Economists Explain,* Cambridge, Cambridge University Press.

Boland, L. (1982) *The Foundations of Economic Method,* London, Allen and Unwin.

Boland, L. (1985) 'Comment on the foundations of econometrics, are there any?', *Econometric Reviews,* 4, 63–8.

Box, G.E.P. and Jenkins G.M. (1970) *Time Series Analysis: Forecasting and Control*, San Francisco, Holden-Day.

Box, G.E.P. and Tiao, G.C. (1973) *Bayesian Inference in Statistical Analysis*, Reading, Addison-Wesley.

Bridge, J.L. (1971) *Applied Econometrics,* Amsterdam, North Holland.

Brunner, K. (ed.) (1972) *Problems and Issues in Current Econometric Practice*, Columbus, Ohio, The Ohio State University.

Cairnes, J.E. (1875) *The Character and Logical Method of Political Economy*, London, Macmillan.

Caldwell, B. (1982) *Beyond Positivism: Economic Methodology in the Twentieth Century*, London, Allen and Unwin.

Chalmers, A.F. (1980) *What is this Thing called Science?*, Milton Keynes, The Open University Press.

Chawdhury, A.R. (1986) 'Vector autoregressions as an alternative macro-modelling technique', *Bangladesh Development Studies*, 14, 21–32.

Chow, G.C. (1966) 'On the long-run and short-run demand for money', *Journal of Political Economy*, 8, 183–199.

Christ C.F. (1952) 'History of the Cowles Commission', in *Economic Theory and Measurement: A Twenty Year Research Report, 1932–1952*, Chicago, Cowles Commission for Research in Economics.

Christ, C.F. (1966) *Econometric Models and Methods*, New York, John Wiley.

Christ, C.F. (1975) 'Judging the performance of econometric models of the U.S. economy', *International Economic Review*, 16, 54–74.

Christ, C.F. (1985) 'Early progress in estimating quantitative economic relationships in America', *American Economic Review*, 75, 39–52.

Cochrane, D. and Orcutt, G.H. (1949) 'Application of least squares regression to relationships containing auto-correlated error terms', *Journal of the American Statistical Association*, 44, 32–61.

Coghlan, R.T. and Jackson, P.T. (1979) 'The UK personal savings ratio: past, present and future', *Scottish Journal of Political Economy*, 26, 307–23.

Cooley, T.F. and LeRoy, S.F. (1981) 'Identification and estimation of money demand', *American Economic Review*, 71, 825–43.

Cooley, T.F. and LeRoy, S.F. (1985) 'Atheoretical macroeconometrics; a critique', *Journal of Monetary Economics*, 16, 283–308.

Cooper, R.L. (1972) 'The predictive performance of quarterly econometric models of the United States', in Hickman, B.G. (ed.) *Econometric Models of Cyclical Behaviour*, Studies in Income and Wealth 36, 2, 813–925.

Courakis, A.S. (1978) 'Serial correlation and a Bank of England study of the demand for money', *Economic Journal*, 88, 537–48.

Currie, D.A. (1981) 'Some long run features of dynamic time series models', *Economic Journal*, 91, 704–15,

Cuthbertson, K. (1985) *Supply and Demand for Money*, Oxford, Basil Blackwell.

Darnell, A.C. (1981) 'A.L. Bowley, 1869–1957', in O'Brien, D.P. and Presley, J.R. (eds) *Pioneers of Modern Economics in Britain*, London, Macmillan Press, 140–74.

Darnell, A.C. (1984) 'Economic Statistics and Econometrics' in O'Brien D.P. and J. Creedy, (eds) *Economic Analysis in Historical Perspective*, London, Butterworths, 152–85.

Darnell, A.C. (1986) 'Some observations on autoregressive distributed lag econometric modelling', Department of Economics, University of Durham, Working Paper No. 78.

Darnell, A.C. (1989) '"General to specific" modelling: A methodological perspective', *British Review of Economic Issues*, 25, 53–88.

Davidson, J.E.H., Hendry, D.F., Srba, F. and Yeo, S. (1978) 'Econometric modelling of the aggregate time-series relationship between consumers' expenditure and income in the United Kingdom', *Economic Journal*, 88, 661–92.

Deaton, A.S. (1977) 'Involuntary saving through unanticipated inflation', *American Economic Review*, 67, 899–910.

DeGroot, M.H. (1970) *Optimal Statistical Decisions*, New York, McGraw-Hill.

deFinetti, B. (1937) 'Foresight: its logical laws, its subjective sources', reprinted in Kyburg, H.E. and Smolker, H.G. (eds) (1964) *Studies in Subjective Probability*, New York, Wiley.

De Marchi, N. (1988) 'Popper and LSE economists', in De Marchi, N. (ed.) *The Popperian Legacy in Economics*, Cambridge, Cambridge University Press, 139–66.

De Marchi, N. and Gilbert, C. (eds) (1989) *History and Methodology of Econometrics*, Oxford Economic Papers, 41.

Dhrymes, P.J., Howrey, E.P., Hymans, S.H., Kmenta, J., Leamer, E.E., Quandt, R.E., Ramsey, J.B., Shapiro, H.T. and Zarnovitz, V. (1972) 'Criteria for evaluation of econometric models', *Annals of Economic and Social Measurement*, 1, 291–324.

Dickey, D.A. and Fuller, W.A. (1979) 'Distribution of the estimators for autoregressive time series with a unit root', *Journal of the American Statistical Association*, 74, 427–31.

Doan, T., Litterman, R. and Sims, C. (1984) 'Forecasting and conditional projection using realistic prior distributions', *Econometric Reviews*, 3, 1–100.

Duhem, P. (1906) *The Aim and Structure of Physical Theory*, English translation (second edition, 1962), New York, Atheneum.

Durbin, J. and Watson, G.S. (1950) 'Testing for serial correlation in least squares regression I', *Biometrika*, 37, 409–28.

Durbin, J. and Watson, G.S. (1951) 'Testing for serial correlation in least squares regression II', *Biometrika*, 38, 159–78.

Dyke, C. (1981) *Philosophy of Economics*, Englewood Cliffs, N.J., Prentice-Hall.

Eichenbaum, M. (1985) 'Vector autoregressions for causal inference? Comment', *Carnegie-Rochester Conference Series on Public Policy*, 22, 305–18.

Eichner, A.S. (ed.) (1983) *Why Economics is Not Yet a Science*, London, Macmillan.

Eisner, R. (1958) 'The permanent income hypothesis: Comment', *American Economic Review*, 48, 972–90.

Engle, R., Hendry, D. and Richard, J-F. (1983) 'Exogeneity', *Econometrica*, 51, 277–304.

Engle, R.F. and Granger, C.W.J. (1987) 'Co-integration and error correction: representation, estimation and testing', *Econometrica*, 55, 251–76.

Epstein, R.J. (1987) *A History of Econometrics, Contributions to Economic Analysis*, 165, Amsterdam, North Holland.

Evans, J.L. (1988) 'Adjustment modelling and the stability of the demand for money function', *British Review of Economic Issues*, 10, 49–76.

Fair, R.C. (1987) 'Macroeconometric models', in Eatwell, J., Milgate, M. and Newman, P. (eds) *The New Palgrave: A Dictionary of Economics* (4 vols), New York, Stockton Press; London, Macmillan Press, 269–73.

Feige, E.L. and Pearce, D.K. (1979) 'The casual causal relationship between money and income: some caveats for time series analysis', *Review of Economics and Statistics*, 61, 521–33.

Fisher, F.M. (1961) 'On the cost of approximate specification in simultaneous equation estimation', *Econometrica*, 29, 139–70.

Friedman, M. (1953) 'The methodology of positive economics', in *Essays in Positive Economics*, Chicago, University of Chicago Press.

Friedman, M. (1957) *A Theory of the Consumption Function*, Princeton, Princeton University Press.

Friedman, M. (1958) 'The permanent income hypothesis: Comment', *American Economic Review*, 48, 990–1.

Friedman, M. (1963) 'More on Archibald versus Chicago', *Review of Economic Studies*, 30, 65–7.

Friedman, M. and Meiselman, D.I. (1963) 'The relative stability of monetary velocity and the investment multiplier in the United States 1897–1958', *Stabilisation Policies*, prepared for The Commission on Money and Credit, 165–268, Englewood Cliffs, N.J., Prentice-Hall.

Friedman, M. and Schwartz, A.J. (1982) *Monetary Trends in the United States and the United Kingdom: Their Relation to Income, Prices and Interest Rates, 1867–1975*, Chicago, University of Chicago Press.

Fromm, G. and Klein, L.R. (1973) 'A comparison of eleven econometric models of the United States', *American Economic Review*, Papers and Proceedings, 62, 385–93.

Fuller, W.A. (1976) *Introduction to Statistical Time Series*, New York, John Wiley.

Galileo, G. (1632) *Dialogo sopra i due massimi sistemi del mondo,* English translation (1953) in Drake, S. *Dialogue Concerning the Two World Systems, Ptolemaic and Copernican*, Berkeley, University of California Press.

Geweke, J. (1988) 'Comment on Poirier: Operational Bayesian methods in econometrics', *Journal of Economic Perspectives*, 2, 159–66.

Geweke, J., Meese, R. and Dent, W. (1983) 'Comparing alternative tests of causality in temporal systems: analytical results and experimental evidence', *Journal of Econometrics*, 21, 161–94.

Gilbert, C.L. (1986) 'Professor Hendry's econometric methodology', *Oxford Bulletin of Economics and Statistics*, 48, 283–307.

Goldfeld, S.M. (1982) 'Comment on Sims (1982)' *Brookings Papers on Economic Activity*, 153–7.

Goldsmith, R.W. (1955,1956) *A Study of Savings in the United States*, Vols I–III, Princeton, N.J., Princeton University Press.

Good, I.J. (1985) 'Comment on the foundations of econometrics, are there any?', *Econometric Reviews*, 4, 69–74.

Goodfriend, M. (1985) 'Reinterpreting money demand regressions', *Carnegie-Rochester Conference Series on Public Policy*, 22, 207–42.

Gordon, R.J. (1984) 'The short-run demand for money: a reconsideration', *Journal of Money, Credit and Banking*, 16, 403–34.

Granger, C.W.J. (1969) 'Investigating causal relations by econometric models and cross-spectral methods', *Econometrica*, 37, 424–38.

Granger, C.W.J. (1981) 'Some properties of time series data and their use in econometric model specification', *Journal of Econometrics*, 16, 121–30.

Granger, C.W.J. (1986) 'Developments in the study of cointegrated economic variables', *Oxford Bulletin of Economics and Statistics*, 48, 213–28.

Haavelmo, T. (1944) *The Probability Approach in Econometrics*, supplement to *Econometrica*, 12, 1–118.

Haavelmo, T. (1958) 'The role of the econometrician in the advancement of economic theory', *Econometrica*, 26, 351–7.

Hadjimatheou, G. (1987) *Consumer Economics after Keynes. Theory and Evidence of the Consumption Function*, New York, St Martin's Press.

Hahn, F. and Hollis, M. (1979) *Philosophy and Economic Theory*, Oxford, Oxford University Press.

Hamouda, O. and Rowley, R. (1988) *Expectations, Equilibrium and Dynamics: A History of Recent Economic Ideas and Practices*, Hemel Hempstead, Harvester, Wheatsheaf; New York, St Martin's Press.

Harvey, A.C. (1981) *Time Series Models*, Deddington, Philip Allan.

Hatanaka, M. and Odaki, M. (1983) 'Policy analyses with and without a priori conditions', *Economic Studies Quarterly* (Japan), 34, 193–210.

Hausman, D. (1981) *Capital, Profits and Prices: An Essay in the Philosophy of Economics*, New York, Columbia University Press.

Hausman, D. (1984) (ed.) *The Philosophy of Economics: An Anthology*, Cambridge, Cambridge University Press.

Hebden, J. (1983) *Applications of Econometrics*, Deddington, Philip Allan.

Hempel, C.G. (1942) 'The function of general laws in history', *Journal of Philosophy*, reprinted in Feigl, H. and Sellars, W. (eds) (1949) *Readings in Philosophical Analysis*, New York, Appleton-Century-Crofts, 459–71.

Hempel, C.G. and Oppenheim, P. (1948) 'Studies in the logic of explanation', *Philosophy of Science*, reprinted (with a postscript) in Hempel C.G. (1965) *Aspects of Scientific Explanation*, New York, Free Press, 245–95.

Hendry, D.F. (1979) 'Predictive failure and econometric modelling in macroeconomics: the transactions demand for money', in Ormerod, P. (ed.) *Economic Modelling*, London, Heinemann, 217–42.

Hendry, D.F. (1980) 'Econometrics – alchemy or science?', *Economica*, 47, 387–406.

Hendry, D.F. (1983) 'Econometric modelling: the "consumption function" in retrospect', *Scottish Journal of Political Economy*, 30, 193–220.

Hendry, D.F. (1985) 'Monetary economic myth and econometric reality', *Oxford Review of Economic Policy*, 1, 72–83.

Hendry, D.F. (1986) 'Econometric modelling with cointegrated variables: an overview', *Oxford Bulletin of Economics and Statistics*, 48, 201–12.

Hendry, D.F. and Ericsson, N.R. (1983) 'Assertion without empirical basis: an econometric appraisal of *Monetary Trends*', Bank of England, Panel of Academic Consultants Panel Paper, No.22.

Hendry, D.F. and Mizon, G.E. (1978) 'Serial correlation as a convenient simplification, not a nuisance', *Economic Journal*, 88, 549–63.

Hendry, D.F. and Richard, J-F. (1982) 'On the formulation of empirical models in dynamic econometrics', *Journal of Econometrics*, 20, 3–33.

Hendry, D.F. and Richard, J-F. (1983) 'The econometric analysis of economic time series', *International Statistical Review*, 51, 3–33.

Hicks, J.R. (1979) *Causality in Economics*, Oxford, Basil Blackwell.

Hollis, M. and Nell, E. (1975) *Rational Economic Man: A Philosophical Critique of Neo-Classical Economics*, Cambridge, Cambridge University Press.

Houthakker, H.S. (1958a) 'The permanent income hypothesis: A review article', *American Economic Review*, 48, 396–404.

Houthakker, H.S. (1958b) 'The permanent income hypothesis: Reply', *American Economic Review*, 48, 991–3.

Hsiao, C. (1985) 'Benefits and limitations of panel data', *Econometric Reviews*, 4, 121–74, and discussion 175–89.

Hume, D. (1748) *An Inquiry Concerning Human Understanding*, reprinted 1955, Indianapolis, Bobbs-Merrill.

Hutchison, T. (1938) reprinted 1965, *The Significance and Basic Postulates of Economic Theory*, New York, Kelly.

Hutchison, T. (1977) *Knowledge and Ignorance in Economics*, Chicago, University of Chicago Press.

Hutchison, T. (1978) *On Revolutions and Progress in Economic Knowledge*, Cambridge, Cambridge University Press.

Hutchison, T. (1981) *The Politics and Philosophy of Economics: Marxians, Keynesians and Austrians*, Oxford, Basil Blackwell.

International Economic Review (1974, 1975) 'Symposium: Econometric Model Performance: Comparative simulation studies of models of the US economy', 15,16, 2 vols.

Jeffreys, H. (1961) *Theory of Probability* (third edition), London, Oxford University Press.

Johnston, J. (1958) 'Book Review' of Friedman, M. (1957) *A Theory of the Consumption Function*, *Review of Economics and Statistics*, 40, 431–5.

Johnston, J. (1963) *Econometric Methods* (first edition), Tokyo, McGraw-Hill.

Johnston, J. (1967) 'Econometrics: Achievements and prospects', *The Three Banks Review*, 73, 3–22.

Johnston, J. (1972) *Econometric Methods* (second edition), Tokyo, McGraw-Hill.

Johnston, J. (1984) *Econometric Methods* (third edition), Tokyo, McGraw-Hill.

Katouzian, H. (1980) *Ideology and Method in Economics*, New York, New York University Press.

Kenen, P.B. (ed.) (1975) *International Trade and Finance. Frontiers for Research*, Cambridge, Cambridge University Press.

Kennedy, P. (1985) *A Guide to Econometrics* (second edition) Oxford, Basil Blackwell.

Keynes, J.M. (1921) *A Treatise on Probability*, New York, Harper and Row.

Keynes, J.N. (1891) reprinted 1955, *The Scope and Method of Political Economy*, New York, Kelly and Millman.

Klappholz, K. and Agassi, J. (1959) 'Methodological prescriptions in economics', *Economica*, 26, 60–74.

Klein, L.R. (1950) *Economic Fluctuations in the United States, 1921–1941*, Cowles Commission Monograph, 11, New York, John Wiley.

Klein, L.R. and Goldberger, A.S. (1955) *An Econometric Model of the United States 1929–1952*, Amsterdam, North-Holland.

Klein, L.R. and Kosobud, R.F. (1961) 'Some econometrics of growth: Great ratios in economics', *Quarterly Journal of Economics*, 75, 173–98.

Kmenta, J. (1972) 'Summary of the discussion', in Brunner, K. (ed.) *Problems and Issues in Current Econometric Practice,* Columbus, Ohio, The Ohio State University, 262–84.

Koopmans, T.C. (1947) 'Measurement without theory', *Review of Economics and Statistics*, 29, 161–72.

Koopmans, T. (1950) 'When is an equation system complete for statistical purposes?' in Koopmans, T. (ed.) *Statistical Inference in Dynamic Economic Models,* Cowles Commission Monograph 10, New York, Wiley, 393–409.

Koopmans T. and Hood, W. (eds) (1953) *Studies in Econometric Method*, Cowles Commission Monograph 14, New Haven, Yale University Press.

Koutsoyiannis, A. (1973) *Theory of Econometrics* (first edition), London, Macmillan.

Koutsoyiannis, A. (1977) *Theory of Econometrics* (second edition), London, Macmillan.

Kuhn, T.S. (1970) *The Structure of Scientific Revolutions* (second edition), Chicago, University of Chicago Press.

Kuznets, S. (1942) *Uses of National Income in Peace and War*, New York, National Bureau of Economic Research.

Laidler, D.E.W. (1971) 'The influence of money on economic activity – a survey of some current problems', in Clayton, G., Gilbert, J.C. and Sedgewick, R. (eds) *Monetary Theory and Monetary Policy in the 1970s*, London, Oxford University Press.

Laidler, D.E.W. (1977) *The Demand for Money: Theories and Evidence* (second edition), New York, Dun-Donnelley.

Laidler, D.E.W. (1985) *The Demand for Money: Theories, Evidence and Problems* (third edition), New York, Harper and Row.

Lakatos, I. (1978) *The Methodology of Scientific Research Programmes*, Worral, J. and Currie, G. (eds) *Philosophical Papers*, Cambridge, Cambridge University Press, vols I and II.

Latsis, S. (ed.) (1976) *Method and Appraisal in Economics*, Cambridge, Cambridge University Press.

Laudan, L. (1977) *Progress and its Problems: Towards a Theory of Scientific Growth*, Berkeley, University of California Press.

Leamer, E.E. (1972) 'A class of informative priors and distributed lag analysis', *Econometrica*, 40, 1059–81.

Leamer, E.E. (1973) 'Multicollinearity: a Bayesian interpretation', *Review of Economics and Statistics*, 55, 371–80.

Leamer, E.E. (1974) 'False models and post-data model construction', *Journal of the American Statistical Association*, 69, 122–31.

Leamer, E.E. (1975a) 'A result on the sign of restricted least squares estimates', *Journal of Econometrics*, 3, 387–90.

Leamer, E.E. (1975b) '"Explaining your results" as access biased memory', *Journal of the American Statistical Association*, 70, 88–93.

Leamer, E.E. (1978) *Specification Searches: Ad Hoc Inference with Nonexperimental Data*, New York, Wiley.

Leamer, E.E. (1983) 'Let's take the con out of econometrics', *American Economic Review*, 73, 31–43.

Leamer, E.E. (1984) *Sources of International Comparative Advantage*, Cambridge, The MIT Press.

Leamer, E.E. (1985a) 'Sensitivity analyses would help', *American Economic Review*, 75, 308–13.

Leamer, E.E. (1985b) 'Vector autoregressions for causal inference?', *Carnegie-Rochester Conference Series on Public Policy*, 22, 255–304.

Leamer, E.E. (1987) 'Specification problems in econometrics', in Eatwell, J., Milgate, M. and Newman, P. (eds) *The New Palgrave: A Dictionary of Economics*, 4 vols, New York, Stockton Press; London, Macmillan Press, 432–5.

Leamer, E. and Leonard, H. (1983) 'Reporting the fragility of regression estimates', *Review of Economics and Statistics*, 65, 306–17.

Leontief, W. (1971) 'Theoretical assumptions and non-observed facts', *American Economic Review*, 61, 1–7.

Leontief, W. (1982) 'Academic economics', *Science* 217, 104–7.

Lipsey, R.G. (1960) 'The relation between unemployment and the rate of change of money wage rates in the United Kingdom, 1862-1957: A further analysis', *Economica*, 27, 1–31.

Lipsey, R.G. (1963) *An Introduction to Positive Economics*, London, Weidenfeld and Nicolson.

Lipsey, R.G. (1966) *An Introduction to Positive Economics* (second edition), London, Weidenfeld and Nicolson.

Lipsey, R.G. and Brechling, F.F.R. (1963) 'Trade credit and monetary policy', *Economic Journal*, 73, 618–41.

Lipsey, R.G. and Parkin, J.M. (1970) 'Incomes policy: a reappraisal', *Economica*, 37, 115–38.

Liu, T.-C. (1960) 'Underidentification, structural estimation and forecasting', *Econometrica*, 28, 855–65.

Litterman, R.B. (1984) 'Forecasting with Bayesian vector autoregression models', *Federal Reserve Bank of Minneapolis Review*, 30–41.

Litterman, R.B. (1986) 'Forecasting with Bayesian vector autoregressions – Five years of experience', *Journal of Business and Economic Statistics*, 4, 25–38.

Litterman, R.B. and Weiss, L. (1985) 'Money, real interest rates and output: a reinterpretation of postwar U.S. data', *Econometrica*, 53, 129–56.

Losee, J. (1980) *A Historical Introduction to The Philosophy of Science* (new edition), Oxford, Oxford University Press.

Lovell, M.C. (1983) 'Data mining', *Review of Economics and Statistics*, 65, 1–12.

Lucas, R.E. (1972) 'Expectations and the neutrality of money', *Journal of*

Economic Theory, 4, 103–24.

Lucas, R.E. (1973) 'Some international evidence on output–inflation trade–offs', *American Economic Review*, 63, 326–34.

Lucas, R.E., Jr (1976) 'Econometric policy evaluation: a critique', in Brunner, K. and Meltzer, A.H. (eds) *The Philips Curve and the Labor Market,* Carnegie Rochester Conference Series, 1, Amsterdam, North Holland, 19–46.

Lucas, R.E. (1987) *Models of Business Cycles*, Oxford, Basil Blackwell.

Lucas, R.E., Jr and Sargent, T.J. (1979) 'After Keynesian macroeconomics' *Federal Reserve Bank of Minneapolis Quarterly Review*, 3, 1–16.

Lupoletti, W.M. and Webb, R.H. (1986) 'Defining and improving accuracy of macroeconomic forecasts: contributions from a VAR model', *Journal of Business*, 59, 263–85.

Mach, E. (1872) *History and Root of the Principle of Conservation of Energy*, English translation (1910), Chicago, Open Court Publishing.

Mach, E. (1883) *The Science of Mechanics*, English translation (1960), La Salle, Open Court Publishing.

Machlup, F. (1978) *Methodology of Economic and Other Social Sciences*, New York, Academic Press.

Maddala, G.S. (1977) *Econometrics*, New York, McGraw-Hill.

Magee, B. (1982) *Popper*, Glasgow, Fontana.

Mann, H.B. and Wald, A. (1943) 'On the statistical treatment of linear stochastic difference equations', *Econometrica*, 11, 173–220.

Marr, W. and Raj, B. (1983) *How Economists Explain: A Reader in Methodology*, Lanham, Md, University Press of America.

Marschak, J. (1953) 'Economic Measurements for Policy and Prediction', in Koopmans, T. and Hood, W. (eds) *Studies in Econometric Method*, Cowles Commission Monograph, 14, New Haven, Yale University Press, 1–26.

Mayer, T. (1975) 'Selecting economic hypotheses by goodness of fit', *Economic Journal*, 85, 877–83.

Mayer, T. (1980) 'Economics as a hard science: realistic goal or wishful thinking?' *Economic Inquiry*, 18, 165–78.

Mayes, D.G. (1981) *Applications of Econometrics*, London, Prentice-Hall.

Mayo, D. (1981) 'Testing statistical testing' in Pitt, J. (ed.) (1981) *Philosophy in Economics*, Dordrecht, Reidel, 175–203.

McAleer, M., Pagan, A. and Volker, P. (1985) 'What will take the con out of econometrics?', *American Economic Review*, 75, 293–307.

McCallum, B.T. (1983) 'A reconsideration of Sims' evidence concerning monetarism', *Economics Letters*, 13, 167–71.

McCloskey, D.N. (1985a) *The Rhetoric of Economics*, Wisconsin, University of Wisconsin Press; Brighton, Wheatsheaf Books.

McCloskey, D.N. (1985b) 'The loss function has been mislaid: The rhetoric of significance tests', *Amercian Economic Review, Papers and Proceedings*, 75, 201–5.

McNees, S.K. (1982) 'The role of macroeconometric models in forecasting and policy analysis in the United States', *Journal of Forecasting*, 1, 37–48.

Meyer, P.L. (1971) *Introductory Probability and Statistical Applications* (second edition), Reading, Addison-Wesley.

Mill, J.S. (1836) *On the Definition of Political Economy*, reprinted in Robson, J.M. (1967) (ed.) *Collected Works, Essays on Economy and Society*, Toronto, University of Toronto Press, vol. 4.

Mill, J.S. (1843) *A System of Logic: Ratiocinative and Inductive*, London, Longmans, Green.

Mizon, G.E. (1977) 'Model selection procedures', in Atis, M.J. and Nobay, A.R. (eds) *Studies in Modern Economic Analysis*, Oxford, Basil Blackwell, 97–120.

Morgan, M.S. (1989) *The History of Econometric Ideas*, Cambridge, Cambridge University Press.

Morgan, T. (1988) 'Theory versus empiricism in academic economics: update and comparisons', *Journal of Economic Perspectives*, 2, 159–64.

Morrison, D.E. and Henkel, R.E. (1970) *The Significance Test Controversy*, Chicago, Aldine Publishing Company.

Nelson, C.R. (1972) 'The prediction performance of the FRB–MIT–Penn model of the US economy', *American Economic Review*, 62, 902–17.

Nelson, C.R. and Plosser, C.I. (1982) 'Trends and random walks in macroeconomic time series', *Journal of Monetary Economics*, 10, 139–62.

Neyman, J. (1934) 'On two different aspects of the representative method', and 'Discussion', *Journal of the Statistical Society*, 97, 558–625.

O'Brien, D.P. (1988) *Lionel Robbins*, Basingstoke, Macmillan.

Orcutt, G.H. (1952) 'Towards a partial redirection of econometrics', *Review of Economics and Statistics*, 34, 195–200.

Pagan, A.R. (1984) 'Model evaluation by variable addition', in Hendry, D.F. and Wallis, K.F. (eds) *Econometrics and Quantitative Economics*, Oxford, Basil Blackwell, 103–34.

Pagan, A. (1987) 'Three econometric methodologies: a critical appraisal', *Journal of Economic Surveys*, 1, 3–24.

Pagan, A. (1988) 'Comment on Poirier: Dogma or doubt', *Journal of Economic Perspectives*, 2, 153–8.

Pesaran, M.H. (1985) 'Comment on the foundations of econometrics, are there any?', *Econometric Reviews*, 4, 75–80.

Pesaran, M.H. (1987a) *The Limits to Rational Expectations*, Oxford, Basil Blackwell.

Pesaran, M.H. (1987b) 'Econometrics', in Eatwell, J., Milgate, M. and Newman, P. (eds) *The New Palgrave: A Dictionary of Economics* (4 vols), New York, Stockton Press; London Macmillan Press, 9–22.

Pesaran, M.H. and Pesaran, B. (1987) *Data-Fit. An Interactive Econometric Software Package*, Oxford, Oxford University Press.

Phelps Brown, E.H. (1972) 'The underdevelopment of economics', *Economic Journal*, 82, 1–10.

Pitt, J. (ed.) (1981) *Philosophy in Economics*, Dordrecht, Reidel.

Plosser, C. and Schwert, C.W. (1978) 'Estimation of a noninvertible moving average process: the case of over-differencing', *Journal of Econometrics*, 6, 199–216.

Poincaré. H. (1902) *Science and Hypothesis*, English translation (1905), New York, Science Press.

Poincaré, H. (1905) *The Value of Science*, English translation (1907), New York, Science Press.

Poincaré, H. (1909) *Science and Method*, English translation (1952), New York, Dover Publications.

Poirier, D.J. (1988a) 'Frequentist and subjectivist perspectives on the problems of model building in economics', *Journal of Economic Perspectives*, 2, 121–44.

Poirer, D.J. (1988b) 'The subjectivist response', *Journal of Economic Perspectives*, 2, 167–70.

Popper, K.R. (1934) *Logik der Forschung* (translated as *The Logic of Scientific Discovery*).

Popper, K.R. (1968) *The Logic of Scientific Discovery* (second edition), London, Hutchison.

Popper, K.R. (1972) *Objective Knowledge. An Evolutionary Approach*, London, Oxford University Press.

Popper, K.R. (1976) *The Unended Quest. An Intellectual Biography*, London, Fontana.

Ramsey, F.P. (1926) 'Truth and Probability' reprinted in Kyburg, H.E. and Smolker, H.G. (eds) (1964) *Studies in Subjective Probability*, New York, Wiley.

Rao, P. and Miller, R.L. (1971) *Applied Econometrics*, Belmont, Wadsworth.

Robbins, L. (1932) *An Essay on the Nature and Significance of Economic Science*, London, Macmillan.

Rose, A.K. (1985) 'An alternative approach to the American demand for money', *Journal of Money, Credit and Banking*, 17, 439–55.

Rosenburg, A. (1976) *Microeconomic Laws: A Philosophical Analysis*, Pittsburgh, University of Pittsburgh Press.

Rust, J. (1988) 'Comment on Poirier: The subjective perspective of a "spiritual Bayesian"', *Journal of Economic Perspectives*, 2, 145–52.

Sachs, J.D. (1982) 'Comment on Sims (1982)', *Brookings Papers on Economic Activity*, 157–62.

Salmon, M. (1982) 'Error correction mechanisms', *Economic Journal*, 92, 615–29.

Samuelson, P. (1947) (1983 enlarged edition) *Foundations of Economic Analysis*, Cambridge, Harvard University Press.

Sargan, J.D. (1964) 'Wages and prices in the United Kingdom: a study in econometric methodology', in Hart, P.E., Mills, G. and J.K. Whitaker (eds) *Econometric Analysis for National Economic Planning*, London, Butterworths, 25–63.

Sargan, J.D. (1975) 'Asymptotic theory and large models', *International Economic Review*, 16, 75–91.

Sargent, T.J. (1973) 'Rational expectations, the real rate of interest and the natural rate of unemployment', *Brookings Papers on Economic Activity*, 429–72.

Sargent, T.J. (1979a) 'Estimating vector autoregressions using methods not based on explicit economic theories', *Federal Reserve Bank of Minneapolis, Quarterly Review*, 8–15.

Sargent, T.J. (1979b) *Macroeconomic Theory*, New York, Academic Press.

Sargent, T. (1981) 'Interpreting economic time series', *Journal of Political Economy*, 89, 213–48.

Sargent, T.J. and Sims C.A. (1977) 'Business cycle modeling without pretending to have too much *a priori* economic theory', *New Methods in Business Cycle Research*, Conference Proceedings, Federal Reserve Bank of Minneapolis, 45–109.

Savage, L.J. (1954) *The Foundations of Statistics*, New York, Wiley.

Seidenfeld, T. (1985) 'Coherence, "improper priors", and finite additivity', *Econometric Reviews*, 4, 81–92.

Simon, H. (1953) 'Causal ordering and identifiability', in Koopmans, T. and Hood, W. (eds) *Studies in Econometric Method*, Cowles Commission Monograph 14, New Haven, Yale University Press, 49–74.

Sims, C.A. (1972) 'Money, income and causality', *American Economic Review*, 62, 540–52.

Sims, C.A. (1974) 'Distributed lags', in Intriligator, M.D. and Kendrick, D.A. (eds) *Frontiers of Quantitative Economics*, vol. II, Amsterdam, North-Holland, 289–338.

Sims, C.A. (1979) 'Review of Leamer (1978), *Specification Searches. Ad Hoc Inference with Nonexperimental Data'*, *Journal of Economic Literature*, 17, 566–8.

Sims, C.A. (1980a) 'Macroeconomics and reality', *Econometrica*, 48, 1–47.

Sims, C.A. (1980b) 'Comparison of interwar and postwar business cycles: monetarism reconsidered', *American Economic Review*, 70, 250–7.

Sims, C.A. (1982) 'Policy analysis with econometric models', *Brookings Papers on Economic Activity*, 107–52.

Sims, C.A. (1986) 'Are forecasting models usable for policy analysis?', *Federal Reserve Bank of Minneapolis, Quarterly Review*, 10, 2–16.

Smiley, T.J. (1985) 'Comment on the foundations of econometrics, are there any?', *Econometric Reviews*, 4, 93–100.

Spanos, A. (1986) *Statistical Foundations of Econometric Modelling*, Cambridge, Cambridge University Press.

Stegmueller, W., Balzer, W. and Spohn, W. (1982) *Philosophy of Economics: Proceedings, Munich, July 1981*, New York, Springer-Verlag.

Stewart, I. (1979) *Reasoning and Method in Economics. An Introduction to Economic Methodology*, London, McGraw-Hill.

Stigler, G.J. (1963) 'Archibald versus Chicago', *Review of Economic Studies*, 30, 63–4.

Stock, J.H. and Watson, M.W. (1988) 'Variable trends in economic time series', *Journal of Economic Perspectives*, 2, 147–74.

Streissler, E. (1960) 'Book Review' of Friedman, M. (1957) *A Theory of the Consumption Function, Econometrica*, 28, 162–4.

Swamy, P.A.V.B., Conway, R.K. and von zur Muehlen, P. (1985a) 'The foundations of econometrics, are there any?', *Econometric Reviews*, 4, 1–62.

Swamy, P.A.V.B., Conway, R.K. and von zur Muehlen, P. (1985a) 'Reply to comments on the foundations of econometrics, are there any?', *Econometric Reviews*, 4, 101–19.

Taylor, M.P. (1988) 'An empirical examination of long-run purchasing power parity using cointegration techniques', *Applied Economics*, 20, 1369–81.

Temin, P. (ed.) (1973) *New Economic History*, Middlesex, Penguin Books Ltd.

Theil, H. (1971) *Principles of Econometrics*, New York, Wiley.

Theil, H. (1978) *Introduction to Econometrics*, Englewood Cliffs, Prentice-Hall.

Thomas, R.L. (1985) *Introductory Econometrics*, London, Longman.

Thornton, D.L. and Batten, D.S. (1985) 'Lag length selection and tests of Granger causality between money and income', *Journal of Money, Credit and Banking*, 17, 164–78.

Tinbergen, J. (1939) *Statistical Testing of Business Cycle Theories*, 2 vols, Geneva, League of Nations.

Todhunter, I. (1949, first published 1861) *A History of Probability, from the time of Pascal to that of Laplace*, New York, Chelsea.

Todd, R.M. (1984) 'Improving economic forecasting with Bayesian vector autoregression', *Federal Reserve Bank of Minneapolis Quarterly Review*, 18–29.

Wallis, K.F. (1969) 'Some recent developments in applied econometrics', *Journal of Economic Literature*, 7, 771–96.

Wallis, K. (1973) *Topics in Applied Econometrics*, London, Gray-Mills.

Wallis, K. (1980) 'Econometric implications of the rational expectations hypothesis', *Econometrica*, 48, 49–73.

Walters, A.A. (1986) 'The rise and fall of econometrics', in Anderson, M.J. (ed.) *The Unfinished Agenda*, London, The Institute of Economic Affairs, 115–24.

Ward, B. (1972) *What's Wrong with Economics?* New York, Basic Books.

Webb, R.H. (1984) 'Vector autoregressions as a tool for forecast evaluation', *Economic Review* (Federal Reserve Bank of Richmond), 70, 3–11.

Wickens, M. (1982) 'The efficient estimation of econometric models with rational expectations', *Review of Economic Studies*, 49, 55–68.

Wiles, P. and Routh, G. (eds) (1984) *Economics in Disarray*, Oxford, Basil Blackwell.

Wonnacott, R.J. and Wonnacott, T.H. (1970) *Econometrics* (first edition), New York, Wiley.

Wonnacott, R.J. and Wonnacott, T.H. (1979) *Econometrics* (second edition), New York, Wiley.

Worswick, G.D.N. (1972) 'Is progress in economic science possible?', *Economic Journal*, 82, 73–86.

Yamane, T. (1968) *Mathematics for Economists: An Elementary Survey*, London, Prentice-Hall International.

Yule, G.U. (1926) 'Why do we sometimes get nonsense-correlations between time-series? A study in sampling and the nature of time-series', *Journal of the Royal Statistical Society*, 89, 1–64.

Zellner, A. (1971) *An Introduction to Bayesian Inference in Econometrics*, New York, Wiley.

Zellner, A. (1979) 'Causality and econometrics', in Brunner, K. and Meltzer, A. (eds) *Three Aspects of Policy and Policymaking*, Amsterdam, North Holland, 9–54.

Index